Breaking the Burdensome Yoke:

A Discipleship Course

in

Forgiving and Grieving

Mark and Dallas Henslee

Published by
   Blue Fire Legacy
   Westcliffe, Colorado

Unless otherwise indicated, all Scripture quotations are from the ESV©
Bible (The Holy Bible, English Standard Version©), copyright © 2001 by
Crossway, a publishing ministry of Good News Publishers. Used by
permission. All rights reserved.

NASB--Scripture taken from the NEW AMERICAN STANDARD BIBLE©,
Copyright © 1960, 1962, 1963, 1968, 1971, 1972, 1973, 1975, 1977, 1995
by the Lockman Foundation. Used by permission. www.Lockman.org.

Authentic Faith by Gary Thomas Copyright © 2002 by Gary L.
Thomas. Used by permission of Zondervan www.zondervan.com
A Grief Observed by C.S. Lewis Copyright © 1961 by N. W. Clerk, restored
1996 C.S. Lewis Pte. Ltd. Used by permission of Zondervan
www.zondervan.com

To protect the privacy of individuals whose stories are told in this book, permission has been obtained to share the stories, or names and identifiers have been removed from the accounts.

Copyright © 2021 Mark and Dallas Henslee

Cover Design Photo: Saikiran Kesari taken from Unsplash.com, used with written permission, and Dallas Henslee, photographs modified.
Cover Layout: Dallas Henslee
Interior Graphic Design and Illustrations: Akilah Picou
Back Cover Author Photograph: Cathy Troyer

ISBN 978-0-9989548-2-0

All rights reserved. With the exception of using a short quote of 50 words or less to promote the teachings presented in this book, no part of this book may be reproduced, stored in a retrieval system, or transmitted in any form or by any means--electronic, mechanical, photocopy, recording, or otherwise--without prior written permission of the copyright owner. All promotional quotes should provide credits including title and authors. Please direct your inquiries to info@bluefirelegacy.org.

In *Breaking the Burdensome Yoke: A Discipleship Course in Forgiving and Grieving*, Mark & Dallas Henslee have produced a book that introduces and assists the reader to both know and have concrete steps to take in living with these issues. Their writing style is interactive and indeed often makes one feel like we are sitting in the same room with the authors. They are clearly not writing from some theoretical position on the subjects as they share clearly and honestly how they have dealt with the subject matter, sharing both their failures and lessons learned.

This study will go far to equip the reader with both a way to get into and know there are steps we can take, when confronted with the subjects of forgiveness and grief. We don't have to be stuck with the weight of not dealing with them - indeed there is hope! Thank you Dallas and Mark for helping to unstick us and assisting us to move ahead with life.

    Dale Schlafer, Center for World Revival & Awakening

I found *Breaking the Burdensome Yoke* easy to read and very insightful. The use of the parable of the unforgiving servant was especially poignant and made me wonder if the book would be better entitled "Finding the way to freedom from the jail cell of unforgiveness and hurt". The book helped me take responsibility for dealing with my own hurts which also deprives Satan of the opportunity to use them for evil, and helped me to deepen my trust in our loving Father.

    Dr. Caroline Brown, Director, WEC International (Canada)

Mark & Dallas clearly have a heart for people, particularly those in leadership. What they share in these pages would be of great value to those who are going through trials. The book is aided by the fact that they speak from personal experience as well as a Biblical perspective.

> Peter and Lynne Yeoman, Pastor, South Wales

Having counseled vocational people-helpers for more than 25 years, I am convinced that the regular and ongoing practice of "forgiveness" is an essential ingredient if one is to have joy in life. The more we care for others, the greater the need to cultivate forgiveness. Mark and Dallas address the challenges in the fundamental process of forgiveness in a practical, reasonable and realistic way.

> Denny Howard, Coach & Clinical Counselor, Creator & Founder of Livstyle LLC Assessments, Director of Netlink Consulting

Forgiveness is one of the most needed messages in the body of Christ today. The principles put forth here are not untested theories, but have seen life changing results in countless lives including ours. Thank you Mark and Dallas for helping us process forgiveness and grief and for many others whose lives will be radically changed through this book.

> Steve and Marci Fish, Senior Pastors, Convergence Church, Fort Worth, TX

In *Breaking the Burdensome Yoke*, Mark and Dallas provide practical guidance for personal inner healing and for walking with others in their process of healing. I have been able to apply the forgiveness and grief principles to my own life and will use them as I invest in the lives of cross-cultural missionaries.

> Nate Slabach, VP of Staff Care, Students International

God has clearly blessed Mark and Dallas with a vision. This book is such a helpful tool in understanding the effects of grief and what true forgiveness looks like. I highly recommend this book for anyone in relationships with others.

> Dave Claeys, Pastor, St. Croix Christian Church, USVI

For anyone struggling with how to forgive and grieve in a healthy way, this is the book for you. Mark and Dallas share in a powerful way both from their own personal experience, combined with what they have learned in ministering to others over the years. As a Licensed Mental Health Counselor for over twenty years, I have seen unresolved forgiveness and grief as major contributing factors to mental health issues, especially addictions. I highly recommend this book both to leaders and lay people in need of healing.

> Gregory Hasek MA/MFT, Licensed Mental Health Counselor, Executive Director, Southwest Florida Christian Counseling

Mark and Dallas Henslee have done a superb job of intertwining scriptural truths about forgiveness and grief with practical steps which lead one to emotional and spiritual health. For someone who recently lost a parent, I found the book extremely helpful, and I believe it will be a benefit to many.

> Rob Woods, Global Group Development Director, Barnabas Ministries, Inc.

Mark and Dallas have done an exceptional job in dealing with a very critical issue. This book is a very practical work as it relates to forgiveness and grieving. Practical insights and applications will help the reader work through the process of healing from a Biblical perspective. I wholeheartedly recommend this fine work.

> Glenn Shock, Pastor, First Baptist Church, Westcliffe, CO

All of us experience emotional hurt and pain in our lives. Often leaving us with more questions than answers. *Breaking the Burdensome Yoke: A Discipleship Course in Forgiving and Grieving* is a practical and powerful book that will give you the tools and encouragement to walk in victory and rest in the arms of our Lord and Savior.

> Dane Caldwell, LINC-UP Missions, Brazil

Come to me, all who labor and are heavy laden, and I will give you rest. Take my yoke upon you, and learn from me, for I am gentle and lowly in heart, and you will find rest for your souls. For my yoke is easy, and my burden is light.

Jesus Christ

Matthew 11:28-30

Table of Contents

Acknowledgements xi

Disclaimers xii

Prayer xiv

Preface xv

Section 1 Forgiveness

1. Why Do We Need to Forgive? 19

2. What is Forgiveness? 35

3. Who Do We Need to Forgive? 51

4. How Do I Forgive? 65

5. I Thought I Forgave, but I'm Stuck 83

Section 2 Grief

6. Grief and Loss 95

7. Individual Process 111

8. The Emotional Web of Grief 125

9. Strategies for Grieving 137

10. Trauma 151

11. Walking in Freedom and Grace 165

Appendix

Common Questions about Forgiveness and Grief 175

Acknowledgements

To our Lord and Savior, we stand in awe and humility that You would task us with such a vast responsibility to teach Your Bride. Thank you for walking with us each step of the way.

To the many clients who have trusted us with your burdens and broken hearts, thank you for permitting us to join you in your journey. We have learned from you how to better communicate what forgiveness *is*, and what it *is not*. We consider it a privilege to be able to rejoice with you as you walk out your freedom.

To the many volunteers who have provided input as we have worked to craft an easy to understand and applicable presentation of forgiveness and grief work, thank you for encouraging us to share more of our personal experiences to help light the path for those behind us.

Disclaimers

While we utilize quotes from other works, please understand a quote does not imply that we endorse or are necessarily in total agreement with all works, ideas, and ideologies represented by the authors cited. You may find that you disagree with some of our positions. We are simply sharing what we have learned to this point, and we recognize that, as we grow in Christ, our understanding continues to deepen. It is very important, even with our material, that you compare all teaching to the inerrant Word of God, the Holy Bible.

Both Mark and Dallas are ordained ministers, and it is from a Christian perspective that we present the following information. While Dallas is a Licensed Professional Counselor in the state of Colorado, the subjects discussed in the following pages are provided within the boundaries of spiritual development and should not be regarded as receiving advice or services from a Licensed Professional Counselor.

We have purposely written this book in a conversational style. We realize that means we've gone against some of the formal English writing rules. For those of you that this creates some irritation, we ask that you find it in your heart to forgive us. There have been numerous instances where people made a point to thank us for using this style in our prior book, and it has become a part of our brand. Above a consistency in appearance and familiarity, we hope that it makes the information a little easier to read and apply.

Prayer

Lord, as each individual reads this book, we ask that You will be their Comforter and Refiner. We ask that Your fruit of perseverance would be present in their lives and carry them through the portions of work they would prefer to abandon in their humanness. Highlight for them each area that needs to be addressed, whether it be moving from unforgiveness to forgiveness or having the courage to grieve completely and well. Wrap each broken heart in Your loving and protective arms, and pour out Your healing oil on those who are in a period of mourning. Return to them a spirit of gladness. Thank You for the freedom You provide as we walk in Your ways.

These things we ask in Jesus' Holy Name. Amen.

Preface

In our work with ministers around the globe, we have found ourselves teaching more on forgiveness than our first book, *Behind Enemy Lines: A Discipleship Course in Spiritual Warfare*, addressed. Therefore, we felt it would be appropriate to expound upon that material. Additionally, we've had people question why the story in the forgiveness chapter of *Behind Enemy Lines* was written as an analogy rather than in a more factual manner. At the time it was written, it helped Dallas to put it in a different context to process the events and grieve.

In all candor, as we began working on this book, we contemplated separating the subjects of forgiveness and grief. This was due in part to the urgency we felt to get the teaching regarding forgiveness printed and distributed as quickly as possible. However, as we began to record what we felt God would have us share with you, we realized that the two are so intertwined, it would be a huge disservice to attempt to address them in monothematic titles.

As the title credit indicates, the material has been written by both of us. This means that there are times when Mark's voice will be more noticeable and others when you will recognize Dallas' style instead. We have largely drawn on our own experiences, although there are a few additional stories strewn throughout the book, which we have included with permission or altered sufficiently to provide anonymity.

Our approach in this book is primarily practical application. There are numerous books with scholarly or Biblical perspectives of both forgiveness and grief. We aspired to provide a different approach for those struggling with the heaviness of dealing with either or both. While our intention is to provide practical information and tools, this is not a self-help book. You will need the help of the Holy Spirit to accomplish the work of healing so that you can walk in freedom.

Should you find yourself in a leadership role in a church that is processing forgiveness and grief issues collectively, we adapt and expand the material included in these pages as it applies to your unique needs. When working in person with church boards and church bodies during painful seasons, including leader dismissal and church body transition, we provide a combination of one-on-one and group sessions.

We pray that you will hear the Lord's still small voice as He indicates each of the areas He wants to discuss intimately with you regarding your brokenness and heavy burdens. Our prayer for you, as you study, learn, seek Him, and do the work, is that you, too, will come to a place of healing, restoration, peace, and proactive discipleship with those around you.

Section 1
Forgiveness

1

Why Do We Need to Forgive?

In 1999, we celebrated Mark's graduation with his master's degree and moved from Texas to Colorado within the span of two weeks. We were excited to be moving to help start a church, even though much of our life was still uncertain. We didn't have gainful employment or housing, just the willingness to take a huge step of faith.

Just four short months later, it was devastating to find ourselves without our start up church where we were to minister. We had both left potential career partnerships behind and uprooted our young family to move across state lines. We found ourselves having to forgive the preacher that we were to team up with during this time.

God continued to grow us during this season of volunteer ministry in another church. Eventually, He told us it was time to step out and be the lead planters for a church in our neighborhood, restoring the original vision. There were many days of prayer asking God what to do next. We met in our home, then we rented various meeting spaces around town for the small group of believers. Through the years, there were Backyard Bible Clubs, block parties, and a larger community event that we facilitated.

Mark's mom moved to live near her grandchildren during this time, and became an integral part of our ministry efforts. She headed up the Children's Ministry and attended to the majority of church administrative tasks. Our world came to a screeching halt when she was diagnosed with cancer and passed away a short seven weeks later. This time, we had to forgive the denominational leaders for not providing any grief care for us, and work through our anger with God that she was gone from our lives so soon.

We carried on to the best of our ability. Contrary to what we teach pastors now, we took one service "off"; although, we still attended. One week of being able to step back from teaching and worship leading responsibilities after having suffered a significant family loss was completely inadequate. Soon burnout was more of an understatement than an accurate assessment of our mental state and emotional capacity to continue in bivocational ministry.

Out of desperation, we approached the denomination and requested that they send another couple to assist us in carrying the load. Unfortunately, they saw this as an opportunity to push us out, which meant that we became the targets of a forced church exit due to earthly ambitions of others. Unless you have been in a similar situation, it would be almost impossible for you to grasp the depth of the hurt and the amount of needed forgiveness and grieving that such events set into motion.

But with God, all things are possible. He redeemed this experience and now we not only empathize with others who have been hurt by the church, we can walk beside them and teach them how to engage in the freeing process of forgiveness.

Obligatory forgiveness and pseudo peacemaking

We can usually spot an obligatory statement or presumption of forgiveness very easily. A similar response is avoidance. We challenge our clients to face each of these issues if we identify them while working together.

Pseudo peacemaking, in the form of conflict avoidance, does not resolve any issue. One can only sweep items under the rug for so long before they are tripping over the mountain that has accumulated underneath. True forgiveness actually cleans the area and makes it possible to carry on without being tripped up.

As referenced earlier, learning how to fully forgive and working through the process is actually a large part of our story in founding Blue Fire Legacy. We had a season of incredibly deep hurts which we had to journey through to be effective in how we minister to others. What we've learned through our personal experience impacts the way we provide ministerial counsel and advise church boards and bodies.

Jesus commanded us to forgive

Before we delve into the process of forgiving, we need to know why we are doing this work. The Lord commanded us to forgive; therefore, we don't have the luxury to dig in our heels and remain in unforgiveness without impeding our relationship with God. Anything that goes against God is sin.

> And whenever you stand praying, forgive, if you have anything against anyone, so that your Father also who is in heaven may forgive you your trespasses. (Mark 11:25)

> For if you forgive others their trespasses, your heavenly Father will also forgive you, but if you do not forgive others their trespasses, neither will your Father forgive your trespasses. (Matthew 6:14-15)

Paul joined with Jesus in emphasizing the necessity of forgiving.

> ... if one has a complaint against another, forgiving each other; as the Lord has forgiven you, so you also must forgive. (Colossians 3:13)

We have been forgiven

Look at that last verse. "As the Lord has forgiven you, so you also must forgive." We forgive because we have been forgiven. How hypocritical would it be of us to receive the Lord's forgiveness and then for us to refuse to forgive others?

Much like the servant in Matthew 18:24, we owed a debt that could not possibly be repaid. Jesus paid *our* debt through His sacrifice on the cross, then He conquered death so that we may live. He expects us to extend to others the same forgiveness that we have received from Him.

If we do not forgive others as we have been forgiven, we are effectively thumbing our noses at God. It is only reasonable that He would then withdraw His forgiveness from us as the master in the parable of the unforgiving servant did in Matthew 18:32-35.

> "Then his master summoned him and said to him, 'You wicked servant! I forgave you all that debt because you pleaded with me. [33] And should not you have had mercy on your fellow servant, as I had mercy on you?' [34] And in anger his master delivered him to the jailers, until he should pay all his debt. [35] So also my heavenly Father will do to every one of

you, if you do not forgive your brother from your heart." (Matthew 18:32-35)

Unforgiveness puts us in a jail cell

To choose to remain angry and offended places us, metaphorically speaking, in a jail cell. We are limited in our ability to experience the fullness of life because this thing, this seemingly impossible to forgive incident, holds us captive. In Matthew 18:34, the unforgiving servant was turned over to the jailers or torturers.

It's hard to imagine a kind, loving God turning us over to the torturers, but that is what is described in this parable. He is responding to our choice which comes with consequences. When we fail to forgive, the Lord will allow the torturers to afflict us until we repent and forgive our offenders. He is allowing it because *we* have been disobedient and in our sin have opened *ourselves* to the torment of the enemy.

Who are the torturers? Sickness, oppression, depression, physical and psychological suffering are some of the torturers that we may be subject to when we choose not to forgive. Our circumstances may seem to be continually against us. It is even possible that the enemy's demons and dark principalities will be allowed to harass us. When the Lord lifts His hand of protection, we are subject to whatever may come our way.

Fortunately, God has given us the key to our own jail cell. The key is forgiveness. We can use it to unlock the door that keeps us entrapped. When we forgive, we are able to receive forgiveness, and we are free from the torturers.

Unforgiveness gives us a distorted view

Let's look at how our perspective can be impaired if we continue to view others through unforgiveness.

The picket fence in the picture represents any offense perpetrated against us. In a state of unforgiveness, we see the other person through the slits of the fence - the fence (or offense) is more in focus and prominent than the person standing behind it.

As we choose to forgive and work through the process, we are pulling pickets off the fence. As we remove each picket, we start to see the offender with more and more clarity. In time, we will be able to pull off all the pickets, the rails, and the posts, allowing us to see the other person without any offense between us.

Remember, the enemy likes to make us think we aren't doing it right when we have to forgive more than once. He's a liar. Don't believe the lies. Forgiveness begins with obedience. In other words, we are bringing our will in submission to Christ's instructions. We'll expand more on the emotional response in forgiveness later, but at the beginning, you may not feel anything other than the need to persevere because you haven't yet found resolution.

Sin gives the enemy strength and opportunity to abuse us

When we choose not to forgive, we are going against the command of God; that is sin. The thing about choosing to sin by remaining in unforgiveness is that we not only allow the offender the power to continue to harm us, but we also hand Satan the opportunity and reinforced strength to abuse us. Anytime sin remains present, the enemy has the right to oppress and torment.

> Be angry and do not sin; do not let the sun go down on your anger, [27] and give no opportunity to the devil. (Ephesians 4:26-27)

When we are hurt, we have a right to be offended and may respond in anger. Anger is a powerful emotion that the enemy likes to twist and use against us. It is common for us to disconnect from our rational thought process when we allow anger to run loose in our life.

We need to take those angry thoughts captive and bring them under control, rather than operating irrationally. We take our thoughts captive when we choose to challenge them, recognizing them for what they are. Beyond acknowledging them, we must look at the point of origination and evaluate whether our response is restorative or retaliatory in nature.

Anger in itself is not a sin; how we display that anger may be

Many have been taught that to be angry is a sin. This is an incomplete teaching. To look at it more fully, feeling anger alerts us that something is wrong. God created us to have and express emotion. The possibility of stepping into sin comes with how we react to our anger. Do we judge? Do we speak ill will toward another? Do we fantasize about or want the satisfaction of revenge? The heart position is the difference between holy anger, which Jesus expressed in the Temple when He overturned the merchants' tables, or human vengeful anger, which is sinful. We can be angry without stepping into the sinful nature.

To hold power and control over another by manipulating them, or meditating on vengeful or judgmental thoughts, is sin. Retaining anger because it gives a sense of power over a situation is a typical human response. We don't like to feel vulnerable or threatened; however, our approach to everyone around us, whether friend or foe, may be impacted by this desire to use anger to "protect" ourselves.

Sometimes we use anger as a motivation to do better in the future. This may be anger at our own actions or those of another. Unfortunately, a negative driving force is still negative.

We must deal with the anger we feel, whether righteous or sinful. One tool that we often use is the Anger Iceberg. This concept has been applied in several different contexts, and therefore, its origin is unknown. For this application, we recognize anger as the more visible alert mechanism much like the top of an iceberg that sticks out of the water.

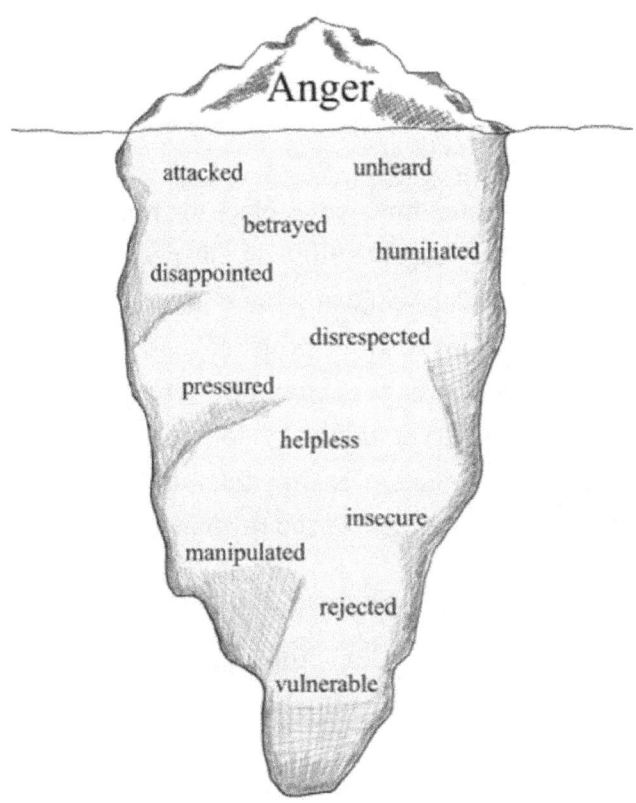

The actual issues that need to be addressed are under the water supporting the anger. As we identify what is submerged or hidden, we can begin to identify the varying supporting elements and find freedom and healing.

Maybe you are angry because someone embarrassed you or impugned your reputation. Perhaps it is even more egregious with someone abusing or stealing from you. Forgiveness work will be needed as you identify each of the underlying issues. It is highly probable that each party has emotional content, wounds, and memories which need to be addressed.

There is a need to move to a place of recognizing that relinquishing the anger strips us of perceived power. Remaining angry can feel like a benefit because it fills the void of feeling powerless. It provides a sense of being in power or control over a person who wronged us in any situation in which we originally felt, or actually were, vulnerable. The problem is that this anger is used as a weapon in the form of fantasized revenge or judgement.

Forgiveness is for our freedom

There is hope and freedom from our hurts. As forgiven children of God, we are not under Satan's rule. In Christ, forgiveness is possible.

Remember the fence analogy from before? As we work through the process of forgiveness, we remove the pickets that are distorting our view. We are removing the rights to remain offended. In this process, we no longer carry the weight of being wronged. We can see the other more clearly. We may even be able to begin to understand why they acted the way they did. Understanding alone does not equal forgiveness, though, so please don't confuse the two. You don't have to understand to forgive, and conversely, you can't always be motivated to forgive through gaining understanding.

We gain benefits from forgiving others

As we read various passages in the Bible that speak on forgiveness, sometimes we mistakenly think that forgiveness is for the offender. Forgiveness is also for our benefit. In the Old Testament, sacrifices were made to provide atonement. With Christ's perfect sacrifice and resurrection from the dead, we no longer have to continually sacrifice animals. We have a choice to receive this gift of forgiveness that permits us to have eternal life in the presence of God.

Forgiveness with our earthly relationships is similar. In Matthew 18:28, we see the unforgiving servant choking his fellow servant. The indication of choking is to take the breath away from someone. Since breath represents life in the spiritual realm, unforgiveness is to take the life away from our offender.

Unforgiveness can also suffocate *us*, choking the breath out of *our* life. We are effectively taking our own life away as we attempt to hold another accountable for the hurt caused. When we choose to forgive, we are removing the stranglehold from our neck, giving us the ability to breathe again. The weight of the offense can be lifted from our shoulders.

Reflection and Review

Reasons to forgive include:

One instance where I remember receiving freedom and release by forgiving someone else is:

Do you have anyone standing with a fence (offense) between the two of you?

Draw your own anger iceberg for the incident that came to mind in the prior question. What are the emotions or negative words that go under the "waterline"?

2

What is Forgiveness?

When our girls were younger, they had received an animated toy dog that went with some other dolls they had. At a playdate, one of their friends was having so much fun with it, she asked to take it home, just to borrow it for a few days. Unfortunately, when she returned it, the toy no longer moved or barked, and changing the battery didn't solve the problem.

This brought about the need to address the grief and disappointment in receiving a broken toy. The friend wanted the act of return to be sufficient to avoid conflict. Of course, for our girls it wasn't, and we had to work through forgiveness with them in this teachable moment.

As children we may have been told to say, "I'm sorry" for any offense or hurt that we may have caused. The statement may or may not have been heartfelt, but we said it to be able to please mom, dad, or another authority figure, and be able to move on to what we wanted to do. A simple "I'm sorry" can become a cop-out and not meaningful. As we age, that pattern of responding to be able to move on may have continued and even still be with us today.

When we work with clients, we use their stories and content from their lives. While we have provided some stories throughout the book, we encourage you to engage your own personal content as applicable in your forgiveness journey.

Many of us have ideas and definitions of what forgiveness means and entails. We have found that it is common to have an incomplete definition, and sometimes, even a misunderstanding of forgiveness. In the next few pages, we will look at what forgiveness is and what it is not.

Forgiveness is releasing our right to be offended

The first step in forgiveness is to recognize our right, or perceived right, to be offended, and then choose to give up or surrender that right. The hurt is real, and we need to recognize the reality of the offense. There is a tendency to minimize the offense, and think that it really wasn't as bad as we originally made it out to be. Other times, we blow things out of proportion. It is important to properly assess the reality of the hurt and its true size.

Forgiveness is releasing our right to hold an offense against another person.

Another way of putting it is to say that they don't owe us anything. We are releasing the person from the debt that was owed. In Matthew 18:27, the master forgave the servant of the debt that he was not able to repay. Jesus used this illustration to point out that when we are hurt by another, a debt has been created that can only be released through forgiveness.

In releasing our right to hold the other accountable for the hurt caused, we step out of a place of judgement and allow God to judge as He sees fit ... without our assistance. When we put ourselves in the seat of the judge, we are actually putting ourselves in a position to be judged in a similar manner (See Matthew 7:1-5).

In releasing our right to be offended, we are **not** saying:

- what the individual or group did was right
- they are absolved from responsibility and consequence(s)
- things will go back to being exactly as they were before the incident
- what the individual or group did was acceptable or permissible
- you surrender the right to exercise appropriate/healthy boundaries going forward

We are simply saying that we value the instructions of our Lord and Savior and are willing to walk into the process of forgiveness. This starts with an act of obedience that will eventually lead to our heart being healed and changed.

Forgiveness is a deliberate choice

God gave each of us free-will to choose whether we will do right or wrong. Forgiveness is commanded in Scripture, and therefore, we need to choose to forgive. (Matthew 18:21-22, Colossians 3:13) The choice is not based on the other person's actions or our desires, but entered into out of obedience to our Lord.

You'll notice later when we emphasize the steps in the process of forgiveness that our statement indicates forgiveness is being chosen, rather than being based on feelings. If we wait until we feel like forgiving, we may never actually do the work. We will simply let the person drift away and sweep the offense under the rug. Denial and avoidance only work so long. Eventually, you are tripping over the mountain of dirt that you have accumulated under your rug.

Feelings are fickle and change easily and often. We'll explore this in greater detail in the chapters devoted to grief. It is our option to bring our feelings into alignment with our will, which is being molded in the likeness of Christ, or to allow our fickle feelings to rule us. If we choose to live based on feelings, we will be like a ship tossed in a stormy sea, thrown to and fro, never finding safety or security on solid ground. Instead, we are to rule over our feelings by choosing to forgive without condition.

Forgiveness is a process

While it would be wonderful if forgiveness were a one-time event, the reality is that we have to walk through the process of forgiving. The deeper the hurt, the longer the process. Having a mental thought of dismissal or saying that you forgive in an overly simplified manner is rarely sufficient to be released fully from the offense.

We commonly advise clients to ask God to show them where they need to work. The best place to start the process is where God highlights. Often, it is quite simply the place you have adequate emotional capacity to start. Occasionally, attempting to look at things chronologically, starting with the initiating event, can cause one to be paralyzed by the enormity of the task. It is permissible to begin working in the middle of the hurtful experience. Unlike a historical event, one does not necessarily need to start at the beginning and work the forgiveness through in exact chronological order. God orchestrates this for the benefit of each individual.

Satan, the accuser of the saints (Revelation 12:9-10), will attempt to convince you that you aren't actually doing the work, or that you're not doing it "right" in those moments the memory pops back up for you to address. He is a liar and not to be believed. Allow yourself the grace to work through the process. As long as you are moving forward, you are progressing and getting closer to freedom.

Deep wounds take more processing than surface wounds. The length of time elapsed does not necessarily equate with the level of discipline and desire to see it through to the end. The key is to work through each piece of forgiveness as able until it is completed. This may require jumping from one hurt to another related offense and back again. We depend on the Holy Spirit to guide us through the process.

We have several illustrations to help you grasp the importance of the process, because differing imagery resonates more with some than others. In addition to the fence analogy, we use a grease jar word picture and also describe the process by using onions as an illustration. We hope one of these images helps you understand that forgiveness is a multifaceted process.

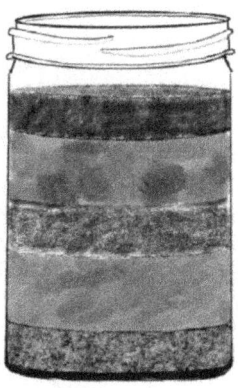

As a visual example, when you pour off waste fat and grease into a jar, you have varying levels of solids and liquid. Once the jar is full, if you wanted to access the liquid at the bottom, for some odd reason, you would have to skim off the solidified fats, layer by layer. Each time you take some off, you are closer to accessing the liquid and emptying the jar completely.

More than one client has pointed out, you're probably dealing with stinky stuff as you work down. True, sometimes we have to face the unpleasantness to get to the bottom of the issue. Forgiving is hard, and there will be times when you have to hold your nose as you work through to the bottom of the hurt.

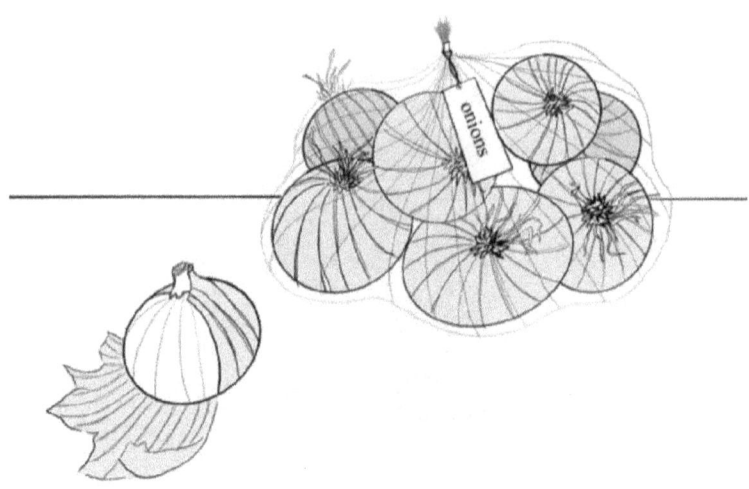

Think about an onion. The outside, dry skin is fragile and easily damaged when bumped. As you move to the next layer, it is a little tougher, and its texture is not pleasing to consume. An onion is made up of many layers which can be peeled off one by one. The outer layers are larger and cover more area than each subsequent inner layer.

When dealing with an offense that requires forgiveness, we will often start with broader, more encompassing thoughts. There may be a layer that is harder and tougher to get through as we begin. Generally, as we work through the process of forgiveness, the details will become clearer, and our forgiveness will be more targeted or specific.

As you peel the layers of the onion, you may find that the gasses released cause you to cry. Crying is often a part of the forgiveness process. Just as water is an important item in our physical process of washing, tears are a part of our emotional washing and healing. We need to acknowledge the emotions we are feeling, and in experiencing them, allow the Lord to wash us with our tears.

The size of each onion will vary depending on the depth of the hurt experienced. There are times that we have multiple related hurts, like a bag of onions. We have to address each hurt until all of the onions have been taken apart and dealt with completely. Don't focus on how big your bag of onions is; instead, take the first one out and start peeling.

The deeper the hurt, typically the longer the process. However, don't lose hope! God doesn't require the same amount of time you have lost in the season of hurt and offense to be expended in healing. He will walk with you through the entire process if you are willing to start and keep going.

Forgiveness is not dependent on others

We choose to forgive regardless of what the other person does or doesn't do. One of the things Mark said to our girls as they were growing up was, "You are responsible for you." In other words, you have to do your part regardless of what the other person does.

That applies here. You don't get a pass on forgiving because the other person is unwilling to change or continues to behave poorly in the same manner over and over. Forgiveness isn't for the other person's benefit. It is for yours. Don't give them the opportunity to hinder your arrival in freedom.

The fact is, you may never get that apology you want. On the other hand, if you get one, you may deem it incomplete, insincere, or insufficient for the offense. You may not get what feels like a satisfactory explanation to you as to why they did what they did or said what they said. Our forgiveness is not dependent on their apology.

It is common for us to have unforgiveness related to offenses from people who are deceased or those we have no ability to contact. Fortunately, we don't have to be in connection with the offender to be able to forgive. Since forgiveness is releasing our right to be offended, we don't have to *receive* anything from the offender.

Forgiving the deceased is not the same as presuming an issue is resolved simply because you will not continue to be in a relationship with them. You still have the choice to forgive things they have done to you in the past, because forgiveness provides healing and freedom for you rather than only being beneficial to them.

Sometimes, we are in a position of hurt with the potential, or even likelihood, that the offender will hurt us again. They may even keep treating you the way they have in the past. That behavior is rooted in their hurt and their past, not yours. Don't get the two confused. These can be difficult places to forgive, but still expected.

On occasion, clients have found it easier to deal with the continued pattern of offense by proclaiming a proactive, inclusive forgiveness statement; basically stating that they choose and purpose to forgive each forthcoming offense that the individual will inevitably hurl at them out of their own unhealthiness. For example, an adult child may forgive a parent for continuing to be critical or unavailable emotionally. Proactively addressing this eventuality creates enough space to deal with each new "assault" as it comes; however, it probably isn't sufficient to eliminate the negative impact in real time. With each new incident, you may find it necessary to use the forgiveness statement we'll discuss in a later chapter.

Forgiveness is placing proper responsibility

In the process of forgiveness, we are to rightly take responsibility or place responsibility where it belongs. The observance of healthy boundaries is permitted; however, blaming is not a part of placing proper responsibility and neither is judgement.

What role did we play in the event that led to the hurt? It is possible that we have responsibility for some portion of the other person's response. They are responsible for their actions, but we may have shared in the process. We need to own our wrongs and not shift that upon others.

Blame shifting can often take pressure off you, but it assigns it where it doesn't belong. Blame is also oppressive in nature and leaves little, if any, room for restoration. Blame is heavy and wearisome to wear. If another shares a portion of the responsibility for things going poorly, approach them, and work things through if at all possible. Don't punish them by assigning or shifting blame in their direction.

Forgiveness moves us away from a position of judging others. Yes, Scripture tells us to know right from wrong and to walk in the ways of righteousness. However, judging someone comes from a heart position of pride and superiority unless God is the one that is judging. The ultimate judgement is His and His alone.

> "Judge not, that you be not judged. ² For with the judgment you pronounce you will be judged, and with the measure you use it will be measured to you." (Matthew 7:1-2)

This verse is often used to exclude all judgement. What if instead it is giving us a warning about *how* we judge others? When we look for faults in others, we will find them. Similarly, they will find fault in us when they look closely. If we choose to look at them with grace and forgiveness, will the Lord then look at us likewise?

To help differentiate approaches, we can apply different verbiage. As Christians, we are commanded to discern right from wrong and choose to live in righteousness. We are to teach our children God's ways. Knowing right from wrong and walking in an upright manner before the Lord is different from judging out of a heart of human comparison and pride.

In contrast to judgement, we are permitted to assign responsibility where it appropriately belongs. Is any of the situation or consequence present because of your own actions, inactions, or words? If so, take your portion of the responsibility. Fess up, and ask forgiveness. You will need to ask for forgiveness from the other person and God.

Asking for forgiveness from someone is not the same as going to someone and saying, "I forgave you for…" In many cases, this is an awkwardly veiled attempt to solicit an apology from an individual who is unaware they offended you. This type of behavior is not restorative, but can cause an even greater issue to address. If they are not aware they have offended you, you may hurt them and create the necessity for them to engage in the forgiveness process towards you for emotionally blindsiding them.

For example, Joe, a disgruntled employee, comes into an exit interview with his employer, Mike. Joe says, "I forgive you for....: and proceeds to make a list of offenses that were not previously brought to Mike's attention, but became so overwhelming for Joe that he felt the need to quit. Mike is now struggling with being a poor employer, even though he had no prior ability to address the list of grievances. A situation such as this also puts Mike in a quandary as to whether to apologize or acknowledge receipt of forgiveness.

Forgiveness is a skill every Christian must master

To walk in obedience to Christ's instructions we must forgive. How well we learn, and practice, the process of forgiveness, will determine our ability to receive forgiveness for our errors and offenses.

Anytime we want to learn a new skill, we have to invest in the process of mastery. We need to study, practice, make mistakes, learn from the errors, practice some more, and keep going until we have mastered the skill. As you learn to forgive, you will stumble at times. Don't give up. Keep working until you have found freedom from the hurts. With enough practice, you can become an expert forgiver, so much so that forgiveness becomes a normal part of your life. We are not purposely looking for offenses so we can practice forgiving. Mastery is about reaching the fullness of forgiveness, not the quantity of things we can forgive.

Humility is required to forgive others and to face our failures as we receive forgiveness. Humility is putting ourselves in submission to the Lord, and thereby lowering ourselves to the place required to forgive and receive forgiveness.

Part of humility is taking responsibility for our actions that have hurt another. If God has convicted you to approach someone to correct a wrong, it may feel more sincere to the recipient for you to say, "I am convicted…" or "I wasn't being kind when I …." Conversely, to start an apology with, "God told me I wasn't…." may feel like you have initiated the conversation without settling your own heart issue with God first.

We forgive in light of our forgiveness received through Christ. Because we have been forgiven, we are able to forgive others. In the next chapter, we will expand on who we need to forgive.

Reflection and Review

The misconception around forgiveness that I have struggled with the most is:

My definition of forgiveness is:

Places I have judged others and need to ask God's forgiveness include:

3

Who Do We Need to Forgive?

Frequently, a client will say, "I had no idea I needed to forgive that! I feel so much better." With practice, you will become an expert at identifying past and present hurts and stepping into a place of forgiveness by addressing specific contributing components.

One thing that tends to trip people up is the need to honor another. Somehow, there is a false notion that to deal with the incident by name and factual occurrence in the context of healing is disallowed because it feels like gossiping. This belief can keep you in bondage. Where do you think that thought process originates? Satan will use whatever he can to steal, kill, and destroy. He will attempt to destroy you, including taking away your freedom, by getting you to stay in a place of unforgiveness by making you think that you can't talk about what happened. Working through a hurt with an authority figure, pastor, or counselor is *not* the same as engaging in gossip. More simply put, motive matters, and working through the details to a place of forgiveness is Biblical.

The other item that frequently keeps people fenced in is applying logic where emotion reigned. Let's look at that a little closer. Offense takes place in our emotions. We may be able to explain it logically with some time, perspective, and additional maturity, but emotionally, we took a hit at the time of the event.

Logic and emotion don't always play well together. It is quite possible that as you speak something out in an effort to begin the forgiveness process that you will instinctively want to recant it, because it doesn't logically make sense. Please don't filter yourself that way. It only keeps you bound.

You may have emotionally time traveled. What do we mean by emotional time travel? Think about a time that you felt you overreacted or someone actually called you out on an overreaction. The thing about our bodies is that they store memory on a cellular level. So, your body reacts to memories just as vividly as real time events. Your brain and body communicate when you are triggered and feel similarly to a previous encounter that mimics the one you are currently in. Emotional time travel is the culprit. See, you aren't just reacting to the current event, but to every time before it that remains undealt with and unresolved. Those layers are what create the over the top response.

You may have better coping mechanisms now than you did at the time of the hurtful event. If the latter is true, it's just as unfair to expect yourself not to need to forgive because of logic or rationalization as it would be to expect a 3 year old to function at the level of an 18 year-old. You didn't have the same information you do now, and your emotions were ignited which caused a response, and encoded in your memory at the time of the infraction.

Of course, it would be all too easy to permit logic to take over and wrestle down emotion through reasoning to a point of never actually working the forgiveness process through. Logic and emotion don't always see things eye to eye. Take care of the emotional distress, even if you can reason through the event or are finding it difficult to find the determination to face down the difficult emotions.

Specifically, when we start looking at *who* to forgive, we teach there are three categories. We need to forgive others, ourselves, and sometimes God. In case that last one tripped you up, hold on, and we'll explain shortly.

Others

This is the area that tends to get the most focus, and the one that most people are familiar with. We can be so hurtful and cruel to each other. Yes, even in the church, this is a sad but true statement.

> "For some reason, we seem more reluctant to forgive fellow Christians than non-Christians, and we are often the most reluctant to forgive pastors and Christian leaders." (Gary Thomas, *Authentic Faith*, page 141).

That's quite an indictment, isn't it? If the world is to know us by our love for each other (John 13:35), we need to learn how to practice active forgiveness, instead of harboring grudges with everyone who offends us. It's okay to hold our fellow believers to a higher standard, including ourselves, but we need to not take that as a license to judge other Christians and separate from them.

There are many things that we need to forgive. The high level obvious offenses are generally easy to identify, but often there are things underneath that we may not easily see. Let's look at some examples so you can better understand looking for the underlying issues that need to be forgiven.

Let's say you had a business partner who mishandled a deal, allocated finances differently than you would choose, or outright intentionally cheated you through deceit or manipulation. What are some of the things you might need to forgive them for? In addition to the misallocation of finances, some possibilities include taking advantage of you, hurting others around you (whether family, employees or clients), lying, harming your ability to trust your judgement, and for taking what didn't rightfully belong to them.

What about a spouse who isn't holding up their part of the responsibilities? Or what if we consider even deeper wounds of a spouse who engaged in an emotional affair, or in infidelity? What might you need to forgive them for other than the obvious egregious offense? A few may be for not considering your feelings, being selfish, making you feel devalued, or showing your children a negative example.

Some of us need to forgive our children. Sometimes, it's for something as significant as ignoring your advice and getting into trouble or taking you for granted. Other times, it may be for breaking your favorite item as they play with it out of curiosity. We are also aware of instances where parents had to forgive their children for scaring them, whether it be for the child getting lost briefly or being in a near fatal accident.

Examples help you start to understand how to evaluate where you may need to step into a place of forgiveness. Hopefully, you are starting to see the pieces. Practice will help you improve. The offense is often deeper than just the presenting issue. Here are a few areas that individuals can overlook or minimize in the forgiveness process:

Forgiving a person for dying

Whether the death was due to old age, accident, or suicide, we may need to forgive the person for dying. Forgiveness is needed even when they didn't choose to die because it left a void in your life, and you miss them. For example, a loved one who died in an accident may need to be forgiven for being in that location, even though they didn't know what would happen. Or you may simply need to forgive them for not being here with you today. This is a place where emotion and logic will likely conflict.

Siblings who were in the womb with multiples that did not reach term may have to address grief and forgiveness issues. There may have already been a bond forming between them in the womb that creates an emotional void in the survivor. This is rarely recognized, because many don't consider the lost baby to have an impact on our life, since they weren't actually born.

Forgiving leaders for not leading well

This one is especially prone to rationalization. Leaders are imperfect people, but you have expressed and unexpressed expectations of them. Personality, skill sets, and Christlike character are just a few of our expectations that may not be met. Some leaders are still learning how to equip their team to grow, and many are still learning the art of delegation. If there's disappointment in your leader, start looking for the specifics you need to forgive, assessing the situation while not judging.

Forgiving others for their expectations of you

We all have expectations of ourselves and others. Sometimes, other people will expect things of us that we don't feel are reasonable or achievable. This can put us in a difficult position of trying to please them while missing the mark. Their expectations may also take away from our ability to achieve our own goals and dreams. This leaves us in a place of being offended by their expectations, leading to the need to forgive.

Self

It's possible that you haven't been taught to forgive yourself. Maybe you got the advice to, "Let it go," but that's akin to sweeping it under the rug without truly addressing it. The Bible doesn't specifically address forgiving ourselves. It doesn't command it, and it doesn't forbid it. So, why, if it goes seemingly unaddressed, do we encourage it?

The enemy can quickly turn unforgiveness of ourselves into self-condemnation, guilt, and shame. None of those are of God. In fact, the Scripture says, "There is therefore now no condemnation for those who are in Christ Jesus (Romans

8:1). That means **no** condemnation from God, others, or ourselves.

It is very common for us to hold ourselves to a higher standard than we expect from others. We should know better, be better, or do more. And yet, we fail on a regular basis. Just as we need to be gracious to others in their shortcomings, we need to show ourselves grace when we fall short.

It is possible that you let yourself down in areas of yearly goals, academic potential, and career dreams. There are so many possibilities here, we won't even attempt to capture them all for your consideration. If you feel disappointed in yourself for any reason, spend time discovering what you are holding against yourself, and work towards forgiving one of the hardest people to forgive - yourself.

You may have not only missed the mark in regard to personal goals and ambitions, but you may feel responsible for neglecting to respond in a situation which you now deeply regret. It is not uncommon for individuals to struggle to forgive themselves if they did not intervene or rescue siblings from abuse, man-made, or natural disasters. It is impossible to undo the past; however, God can provide freedom from guilt when you choose to forgive yourself, in addition to requesting His forgiveness for your prior inaction.

Something else to ponder. You ask God to forgive you because you take Him at His word that He will forgive. How is it then that you feel justified in choosing not to forgive yourself? Do you know something that God doesn't know about the situation that merits not forgiving yourself? The moment you decide to place yourself in opposition to God, you are guilty of sinning. If He forgave you, but you didn't forgive yourself, you have, possibly naively and unknowingly, put your judgement in higher authority than His. The first commandment is pretty clear that we should have no other gods before Him; including the god of our own opinions.

We have found that forgiving ourselves is usually the hardest forgiveness work we have to do. Our pride gets in the way, or we think that we need to feel that hurt just a little longer so we don't mess up again.

That's like keeping a smelly unintentional science experiment that's been unearthed from the back recesses of your refrigerator out on the countertop so you can see it and smell it each time you walk by as a reminder to use up leftovers before they spoil. It isn't necessary to keep a health hazard around to remind you, whether in a physical, emotional, mental, or spiritual context. We can learn from our mistakes without keeping the grotesque trophy.

God

We get some odd looks when we start teaching that there are times we need to forgive God. How can we forgive God when He is perfect? You're right. He is perfect. We don't question that or teach any differently. We also acknowledge that some of you have been taught that the expression of any disappointment or anger towards God is wrong. If you're having a hard time with the thought that we might have to forgive God, give us just a little latitude as we walk you through the foundations of this principle.

It's not that God did anything wrong. He can't, because He's perfect. However, we can perceive, and operate out of, an offense because He didn't do something the way we expected. He didn't sign our prefabricated contract outlining our exact expectations of His performance. It's also possible that we are offended that He didn't prevent or remove us from an abusive, painful, or difficult situation.

Therefore, when we forgive God, what we are actually doing is letting go of our right to be offended that He didn't do something our way. **We are submitting our ego to His will, design, and purpose, and then realigning with Him.** This allows our relationship with God to be reconciled from our position toward Him; His never changed toward us. It is very common for our clients to realize that after they let go of their offense toward God, they need to ask Him to forgive them for their impertinence.

It is easy to transfer the lens of an experience with a human, a fellow fallen creature, onto God; especially if the abuser was male or a father figure. During the process of forgiving God, we may find that there is an offense from a person that we need to forgive. In forgiving God, and the other person, we can see each for who they are in reality.

It is incredibly difficult to reconcile how a loving God could permit suffering, and yet we see it over and over in Scripture. We attribute that to the entrance of sin and death into the world, and while it has been conquered for eternity (God lives outside of time), we are still locked in the system of time until this world comes to an end and His promises will be fully realized.

Sometimes, in the process of forgiving God, we need to throw a tantrum. I know that potentially goes against everything that you've ever been taught about how we need to approach God with reverence and respect. We are not a servant in the King's court who has to follow all of the rules of decorum and protocol under threat of punishment. We are a beloved child that sometimes needs to run screaming into the Throne Room.

When a five year old is hurt, they don't calmly go tell their daddy. They cry and scream. There is a need for us to fall into our daddy's arms releasing *all* of the emotion.

He is big enough to handle every bit of what we feel. Until we allow ourselves to tell Him fully about it, we are allowing the hurt to be a barrier between us and the Lord. He is a loving father who will not turn us away.

Pulling it together

At the beginning of chapter one, we shared a little about our need to forgive in relation to a major church hurt. To help you pull together the concepts of who we forgive with more detail, here is more of our story.

The other people we had to forgive included the individuals who initiated the coup d'état (or as we usually refer to it, the hostile takeover). These were some of the harder, longer forgiveness processes. The pastor who came in to "support" us was not fully honest with his intentions during the initial evaluation meetings, resulting in a lot of forgiveness work on our part. We also had to forgive the members of the church for not asking more questions about what was going on, and for not doing more to protect us.

We had to forgive ourselves for several things. Just needing the help in the first place was something that Mark struggled through. Mark had to forgive himself for requesting the help which led to the takeover. Dallas chose to abstain from the vote that brought in the eventual replacement pastor instead of voting in opposition. We had to forgive ourselves for not fighting harder. These are just a few of the things that we had to work through in our process.

Finally, we had to forgive God for not intervening in the way we expected. It felt like we had been abandoned and left uncared for at the side of the curb. Much work was required in bringing ourselves into alignment with Him.

Whether we are stepping into a place of forgiving others, ourselves, or God, simply put, forgiveness is not for the benefit of the other party; it is for our benefit and healing. Hopefully, that helps you understand the what, why, and who. Next, let's look at the process of letting go of the offense. It's usually more involved than looking at the person and quickly saying, "I forgive you."

Reflection and Review

Who do I need to forgive, and what do I need to forgive them for? You'll come back to this list after reading the next chapter.

Do you have an example of struggling with logic and emotion in regards to engaging in forgiveness?

4

How Do I Forgive?

Whitewashing the offense

Think back to the illustration from chapter one of the fence. Far too often we will paint our fence to look nice, or so we think. This may be the way we justify the offense, or cover it so that it is just a part of the scenery.

A common way we whitewash the offense is through justification. It is easy to rationalize why the person did what they did, especially if we have been prone to such actions ourselves. No matter how good we get at the mental gymnastics of justification, we still experienced the hurt. Our emotions don't think logically, so we need to step out of the rational and into the emotional.

Ignoring the hurt is a way of painting our fence to blend into the landscape. We can pretty it up and make it more attractive, but it is still separating us from complete freedom. Until we remove the offense, we will keep running into it.

We may even learn how to wear our hurt as a badge or medal of honor. Most of us have met someone who is prideful about what horrible things they have experienced and share under the guise of, "Look what I've had to overcome to get this far." While our past is a part of our testimony that God wants to use to help others, we need to be healed in order to most effectively be of assistance to people needing our experience without continuing to perpetrate our hurt.

No matter how you color it, the fence is a hindrance to living life fully. Instead of getting out the whitewash, start taking the pickets off until you've completely removed the fence.

We find that many believers do not know how to engage in the actual process of forgiving. They understand the Biblical principles, but actually doing it is quite another task. Therefore, we teach a process to individuals, couples, and larger groups to assist them in knowing how to forgive.

In this chapter, we will walk through step-by-step the process of forgiveness. Here are the basic steps:

1. Preparing our heart and choosing to forgive
2. Verbalizing the forgiveness
3. Refining and repeating the forgiveness statement as needed

4. Seeing the offender differently and thanking the Lord for the freedom

Step 1: Preparing our heart and choosing to forgive

Before we can forgive, we need to take a look inside our hearts. In order to address the hurts adequately and release our right to be offended, we have to come to a place where we are willing to forgive.

Prepare your heart

At times, we find that a person is not yet at a place where they are willing to release the hurt. They want to be mad about it for a little while longer. It's not really that they want to be mad; it's more that they haven't finished processing the hurt to a place where they can let it go. Effectively, they are stuck in a web of emotions. It's easy to *say* the words of forgiveness, but much harder to *mean* them. Our hearts have to be at a place where we are willing to forgive, even if it is only a choice between surrendering to act in obedience and continuing to live in judgement.

When forgiving ourselves, there is the need to get past the place of paying penance for our failure. There's a misperception that if we forgive ourselves, then we are saying what we did was okay. Alternatively, we choose not to forgive ourselves because we feel that we need the reminder so that we don't make the same or similar error in the future. That's a vicious cycle holding us in bondage that will only end when we choose to release ourselves from the expectation to pay for our failure. Truthfully, we can never adequately repay the cost of the failure.

Choose to forgive

Once we have decided that we are willing to forgive, we need to make the actual choice to forgive. While these are closely related, they are both necessary to find freedom. I can be *willing* to forgive someone and yet remain in unforgiveness because I have not *chosen* to do the work of forgiving.

The choice to forgive is a conscious decision that propels us to put in the necessary effort to work through the process. As we proceed, we may have to choose again, and again, to continue working until we complete the forgiveness process. The choice is an ongoing decision to press through to completion.

Forgiveness is hard work, often emotional, and therefore, we may decide that it is too hard and not worth the effort. We all have the ability to remain in unforgiveness, if that is what we choose to do. It's a bad decision that leaves us tormented, but one that we can elect to make. We recommend breaking out of the bondage and choosing to forgive.

Prepare your space

Having your mind and heart present with intention will likely mean finding a quiet and private place to do the work you've determined to do. Privacy is important, so that you are able to vocalize the forgiveness without concern of being overheard. Don't assume you'll be able to tune out other people, notifications on your phone, television chatter, or music. Lyrics have a way of drawing your mind's attention, as do other conversations. Plan to provide adequate time and a safe environment for yourself as you work through these emotionally intense memories.

Step 2: Verbalizing the forgiveness

We encourage you to speak the forgiveness statement aloud rather than thinking it. There is power in the spoken word, just as there is power in our testimony. Spoken forgiveness combines the elements of the authority and power of our agreement with God's willingness to forgive.

Think about reading some particularly poignant news that impacts you personally. Now, consider what changes for you when you begin to read the very same words aloud. Somehow, it makes it more real, tangible, and emotionally impactful. Forgiveness provides freedom for you as you extend it toward yourself or another. Wouldn't you want the freedom to be as powerful and complete as possible?

We use a process that combines kinetic and verbal components. The pieces are borrowed from various therapy methods which did not originate with us, nor are they unique to us. The kinetic process we use involves tapping on the side of your finger. We'll explain in detail a little later.

We use these components in combination, because the kinetic portion tends to help an individual stay present or grounded in the task at hand, and because the spoken word is powerful. We start with three repetitions because it often takes at least this many times to join one's physical body, mind or emotions, and inner spirit. However, there are times where more than three repetitions are needed.

We frequently observe that the first time someone works through the forgiveness statement and tapping sequence, it is extremely, dare we say even almost entirely, mental. The individual is concentrating on tapping correctly and saying the complete forgiveness statement.

Usually on the second time through, although sometimes this is delayed until the last time through, there is a noticeable emotional release. As we watch the client, something in their face or body language will shift and soften. At times, along with the body language shift, there are accompanying tears. That's part of the process. The tears are carrying stored toxins away.

The last time through can feel as if it simply becomes a matter of fact. The memory becomes a piece of our history that no longer has painful emotion(s) attached to it. We are designed to learn from our memories, therefore, it is more prudent to approach the work from the perspective of dealing with separating the distressing emotion from the memory, rather than having the goal of erasing the memory completely.

The forgiveness statement

The sentence you construct to use for your forgiveness statement needs to be specific rather than general. If you start with something too general, you will likely feel that you need to compose a subsequent accompanying statement to benefit fully from the release.

Think of it this way. When you construct a paragraph, you typically have an overview, supporting evidence, and then review what was presented. Your forgiveness statements are the supporting evidence, rather than the set-up and review. The amount of specificity in each statement will depend upon the detail needed to find completeness in the process.

At the end of each set of repetitions of the constructed statement, take a moment to evaluate what changed from when you started. That will usually let you know if you are done, or if there is more related forgiveness work to address. For larger issues, you may need to set aside time over several days, as attempting to address it all at once becomes overwhelming. If you feel like it is not complete, repeat the statement again, modifying as needed.

The basic statement that we use is: "My subconscious and I choose to forgive (person) for (specific action or inaction)." Some prefer to use "All of me," in place of "My subconscious and I". We've even had one person who used "Me, myself, and I" for the statement. The point is that you are involving all of your being in the process of forgiveness.

One time, we were asked to conduct training for pastors and church leaders overseas that often find themselves in the role of counselor. Because of the language barrier, we utilized a translator.

Earlier that trip, we had taken an area youth group through applicable pieces of the training. As we were working through the forgiveness portion, the young translator looked at Mark as if to say, "I don't know how to translate that word/concept. Give me more info." There wasn't a word for the subconscious in their language. They talked it through enough for a muddled translation.

A couple days later at the pastor training, we decided to use "all of me" instead of "subconscious", because of the difficulty the translator that helped us with the youth group experienced. It was an easier concept for them to understand. We found out afterwards that the young translator was hoping to learn how the seasoned translator would handle the word subconscious and was disappointed when we changed it.

Tapping while forgiving

While you are saying the statement aloud, we encourage you to add the tapping for the kinetic, grounding impact. It has the ability to help one stay present and intentional instead of being distracted in thought. Individuals that need kinetic input (fidget with something like a rubber band, drumming with a finger or foot, need to hold something while talking) usually benefit from the tapping. Try using the tapping for the first few statements. If you truly don't find it beneficial, you can abandon the tapping and use the statements alone.

The diagram below shows which digit to use depending on the entity being forgiven. We use the index, or pointer, finger when forgiving ourselves. The middle finger is used when we discover it is necessary to come into alignment with God and lay down our expectations by forgiving Him. The pinky finger is used for anyone else we are forgiving.

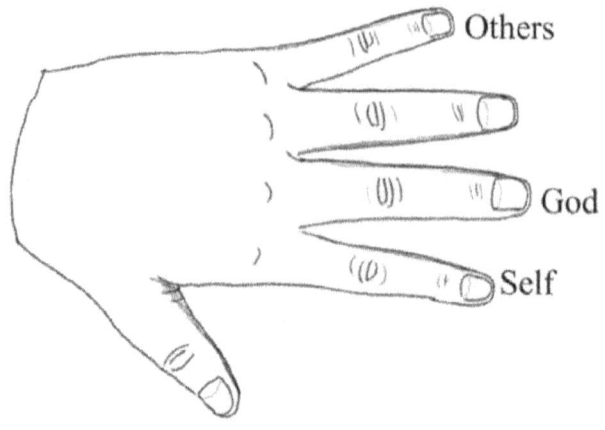

We are often asked why we skip the ring finger. Originally, we were taught, and subsequently taught others, that we skip the ring finger because it is used to complete an internal energy circuit typically employed in Eastern religions. Since then, we have learned there are many different Mudras or hand positions specifically used in Eastern religious practices to awaken the power of the divine as desired. Mudra means seal or closure, and the circuit created with the ring finger and thumb touching is called the Mother Earth Mudra.

We don't have to awaken God's power. It is alive, and if He lives in us, it can continually flow through us. He may choose to anoint us with an additional display of His power at any time of His choosing, but we are submitted to Him, not the other way around.

It matters not which hand you use to tap on the other. You may find one arrangement more comfortable. Use the index finger on one hand to tap on the side of the appropriate digit near the nail bed on the other (see next diagram). You will be tapping and speaking out your forgiveness statement at the same time. We know; it's a little like chewing gum and walking at the same time, but it gets easier with practice.

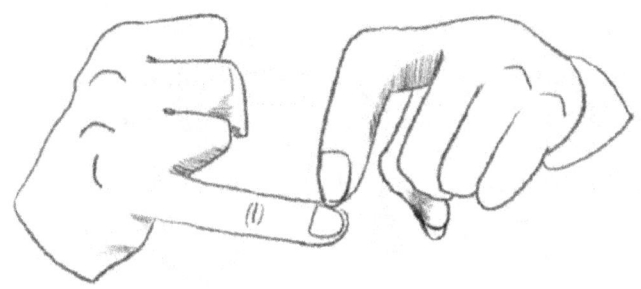

Sample statements of forgiveness

Others: My subconscious and I choose to forgive (person) for (specific action/or inaction).

Alternative statement: All of me chooses to forgive (person) for (specific action).

Tap on the pinky finger while saying the statement out loud.

Repeat the statement aloud three times, or more if needed, for completeness.

God: My subconscious and I (or substitute "All of me") choose(s) to forgive God for (fill in the blank here).

The middle finger is the one we tap when forgiving God.

Say the statement out loud three times, and then assess if you need to repeat, refine, or better specify what you are choosing to forgive.

In the process of forgiving God, you may find places where you would like to ask Him for forgiveness. That is not a tapping, repeated statement space. Rather it becomes a prayer of confession and repentance. No tapping required.

Self: My subconscious and I (or substitute "All of me") choose(s) to forgive myself for (specific action/or inaction).

Tap on the index finger while saying the statement out loud.

Repeat the statement aloud three times, or more if needed, for completeness.

Remember, in all of the above statements, the specificity of the statement will vary based on individual need and intensity of the offense. While we use a standardized statement and tapping, it is important not to be so tied to the method that it systematizes God. Follow His directions if you need to adjust the process.

Step 3: Refining and repeating the forgiveness statement as needed

After we have verbalized the forgiveness, we need to check the remaining level of hurt. This can be done using a simple 0 to 10 scale.

For most, we use the scale of ranking the original hurt as a 10. After each round of forgiveness, we check to see where the hurt is valued currently. The goal is to get the emotional response to the offense down to a zero. You may find that visually going back to a mental picture of the place of offense helps to evaluate the intensity of your current emotional response.

Until you are fully released from the offense, the process is not complete. Each time you verbalize forgiveness, you may find that the statement needs to be adjusted or refined. Remember that the more specific the forgiveness statement, the more likely you are to find release.

It is also possible that there is more than one offense tied together. In these cases, we will require more than one statement to find completeness. Occasionally, you will trigger a completely unrelated offense during the current forgiveness statement. If you are reminded of an unrelated or similar offense, write it down so you can go back to it after completing the hurt you are currently working on forgiving. Don't go chasing after everything in the moment. Proceed with your current content until you have seen it all the way through.

As you peel the onion, you may need to take periodic breaks. This can be a very overwhelming process, both physically and emotionally. By breaking up the process, there is the ability to internalize each step, letting it settle before continuing to the next layer. While breaks are needed, it is important to remain diligent in working through the entire process to completion.

One method we have found to be helpful is to set aside 10-30 minutes each day for forgiveness work. Keeping a running list of items needing forgiveness allows you to not have to remember them, thereby removing the need to keep the offenses continually top of mind as you go throughout your normal daily activities. Each time you sit down to work, ask the Lord to highlight which item to work on that session. When something is complete, cross it off of your list. If you know it needs to be revisited, leave it on the list. If it resurfaces later, write it on your list to address again. Eventually, it will cease to come to your attention because you will have reached a place of resolution.

We have been told that by making a list of things to forgive, it seems we are suggesting that you keep a list of wrongs. 1 Corinthians 13:5 tells us that love "does not keep an account of a wrong suffered" (NASB). When making a forgiveness list, our intent is to do the work necessary to be able to release the offenses. When we have completed the forgiveness work, we will dispose of the lists made, thereby not keeping an account of the wrong.

Step 4: Seeing the offender differently and thanking the Lord for the freedom

As we work through the process and remove the fence pickets, we are able to see the offender differently. With the space opened where we once had a picket of offense, we see the person instead of the hurt. This doesn't mean that the offender becomes a safe person, nor suggest that we are at a place of required reconciliation. It means that we can see them for who they are instead of what they have done.

It is possible to forgive completely and never reconcile the relationship. Some relationships are harmful; we are not required to re-engage in the old patterns. This is where it is important to assess appropriate boundaries. If you can renegotiate boundaries, preserve a portion of your relationship, and both parties benefit from doing so, feel free. However, if there is no way to re-enter the relationship in a healthy way, we recommend that you not allow guilt or shame to draw you back in.

Many of our clients have expressed that they have compassion for the offender, because they can now see the hurt that the person had experienced which led to the behavior causing the offense. Where before they only saw their own hurt, God gave them a clearer vision of what was behind the other person's actions. This isn't justifying what the offender did, but giving an understanding to why they did it.

After finding freedom from the hurts, it is appropriate to thank the Lord for bringing you to that place. He is the Healer and deserving of our praise and appreciation. Worship the Lord in whatever way you feel expresses your gratitude.

Practical example

Sometimes, what we need to forgive seems insignificant because we have moved on with life, and it doesn't continue to plague our memory. Parents frequently discount needing to forgive their children for scaring them because presumably, it comes with the territory.

Let's look at an example and pull out some potential forgiveness statements, so that we can add application to the theory we've already presented.

When we were leading home church, we had several people over for an evening meeting. We had one of those days where parental instruction and discipline were necessary with our oldest, but there wasn't enough time for reconciliation of relationship before everyone arrived. All of the sudden, Dallas realized that we hadn't seen our daughter in some time. There was an urgency about this realization, and we quickly discovered that she wasn't in our house. After suspending our meeting to search for her, she was found a few streets over because she had attempted to walk to her friend's house.

With this brief scenario, what are some potential forgiveness statements that could be constructed? Here's a few ideas to get you started.

- My subconscious and I choose to forgive (name) for scaring me.
- My subconscious and I choose to forgive (name) for running away.
- My subconscious and I choose to forgive (name) for putting herself in a dangerous situation.
- My subconscious and I choose to forgive (name) for causing a disruption.
- My subconscious and I choose to forgive (name) for embarrassing me.

Reflection and Review

Go back to the list in the prior chapter review and create specific forgiveness statements for each.

Can your statements be broken down into smaller details?

Evaluate the distress of the issue before starting the forgiveness statements, and give it a value of 10. After saying the specific statement three times aloud, re-evaluate your distress level attached to this event. Has it come down? Continue until you feel you are at a value of zero.

How are you entering into thankfulness and praise for the freedom the Lord has given you?

5

I Thought I Forgave, but I'm Stuck

Forgiveness is a process, and it is common to get only part way through and think we are finished. As with most things, it's easy to feel stuck before we have truly completed the task. We may have finished pulling down part of the fence, or peeling half our onion. Because we feel better with the progress made, we interpret the partial relief as though we are done.

There are also times when we have to take a break from the process before we are ready, or able, to finish. We may need to celebrate the victory found at that point, or recognize that we do not have enough emotional capacity to deal with the deeper core of the issue without needed recovery time. Allow yourself the grace to recognize what has been done, and prepare to finish what is remaining at the appropriate time in the near future.

When you are feeling stuck in the forgiveness process, you need to step back and evaluate where you are and what needs to change to move forward. Let's take a look at some common places that people get stuck and how to get out of them.

Make sure you really are stuck

Sometimes, it is easy to assume we're stuck because we aren't free yet. Maybe you are mid-process.

Remember the quick tool to assess this is to give the original event a value between 0 - no distress and 10 - the most distress you can imagine. The original event value is 10. Now assign a new value for the level of distress in the current moment as you think back on it. If it has reduced, that is an indication you have completed some of the work, but have not yet reached a point of conclusion. Of course, we desire the value to come down to 0 and the memory to be matter of fact; simply a part of your history without having difficult emotions attached to it.

How do you know if you are officially stuck? The value remains the same intensity between 0 and 10 each time you assess it. Here are some other potential trouble areas that you can consider to create momentum in the healing process again.

Resistance to forgiving

Resistance can sound like, "I'm not ready" or "You're rushing me." There is legitimate grief to be worked through as we forgive. If you are in this stage, you may need a little more time to walk through the grief pieces before stepping into the obedience of forgiveness. We'll delve into the many facets of grief in the coming chapters.

We've been known to ask a client if they are ready to forgive or if they aren't done being mad yet. We can't force them to forgive, even if we make them go through the formality of the described process. To lead them through the mechanics of forgiveness without the heart intent is nonproductive and can lead to frustration.

For example, two children are playing and one grabs a toy out of the other's hand. The small child is told by their parent to return the toy and say, "I'm sorry." The other child is then told to say, "It's okay," or "I forgive you." How much meaning is there really in those words? The children are saying what they are told because they want to move on with playing. Adults will often follow this same pattern with forgiveness. We need to step back and determine our true motivation and adjust as needed to get to a place where we are ready and willing to forgive.

Putting conditions on forgiveness

Putting conditions on forgiveness renders it ineffective. When we establish conditions in this process, we agree with Satan to warp what God intended.

Forgiveness is not based on the other person's response, or the offending individual accepting and taking responsibility. Out of our desire to re-establish relationship, often on our terms, we get ourselves ensnared in a trap of the enemy.

Unlike asking for forgiveness because we are aware that we have hurt someone, extending forgiveness does not involve *telling* the other party what we are forgiving them for at our own initiative. When we step into this place, we are no longer working in a space of freedom and release. Rather, we shift the discomfort from ourselves to the other person and weaponize a twisted version of forgiveness. This is where wounds are created and deepened rather than healed.

If you feel the need to tell the offender what you are forgiving them for, please ONLY do so to an empty chair during a time that you have complete privacy. The purpose of the chair is to represent the person in absentia (For more about the empty chair, see chapter nine page 138).

Is the forgiveness statement specific?

Have you thought through the event completely, identifying each part that was difficult for you? We have found that the more specific the forgiveness statement, the more effective it becomes. It is important to break the statements down into bite sized pieces, so to speak. In our urgency to feel better, occasionally we try to lump everything together or be overly general in our statement. What we wind up with is a long, complex statement, rather than a succinct 3-5 word phrase.

We also find it common to lump several individuals together in one forgiveness statement. Try forgiving each person by name, or role if you cannot recall their name, rather than by a group identity. There are occasions when it is more appropriate to forgive as a large group, but this is the exception rather than the rule. As we forgive, we are releasing our right to be offended by each individual.

Are you vocalizing forgiveness?

Are you saying the forgiveness statements aloud? As discussed in the prior chapter, there is more power in speaking out the forgiveness statement than just thinking it in your mind. It becomes more real and powerful when you vocalize the words. Are you giving voice to your intent and hearing yourself do so?

Did you repeat the statement three times to allow each part of your being to resonate with it? We often find people initially resistant to the repetition of the statements. This could be because they mean it the first time and don't see why it needs to be said again, or they want to hurry up and be done with the forgiveness so they can go on with more enjoyable things. To find the fullness of forgiveness, we need to put in the time, effort and emotional investment through the entire process.

Is there a distraction?

Be sure that you have eliminated potential distractions and given yourself a safe space to work. You want forgiveness work to be freeing, not an anxiety producing effort to perform the forgiveness statement "just right".

If you are more focused on the tapping and the statement than the actual substance of the work at hand, try placing your finger on the appropriate digit and holding it there rather than tapping. For some, tapping is not helpful, and they can simply say the forgiveness statements.

It is more important to have your mind and heart engaged in the process than to just do the exercise "right". The Lord is looking at your heart's intent and will honor your effort when done with the correct motivation.

Most people need to limit the amount of time working on forgiveness in each session. The emotional investment is significant, and we want to be sure that we have full engagement throughout the process. We are not in a race to finish; we want to complete the work needed for full freedom. Some find it beneficial to dedicate a certain amount of time each day until they have completed working through their list. A reasonable amount of time varies for each individual, but we recommend 10-30 minutes daily.

Are you emotionally time traveling?

We discussed the possibility of difficult situations or traumatic experiences fusing together in an earlier chapter. (See page 52 for a refresher if needed). You may be having a hard time coming to a point of conclusion because you are triggered and have forgiveness work to do on a related or similar event involving different people. Do a little detective work, and see if this is why you feel stuck.

We recommend that you have a notepad handy as you work through forgiveness. Often, the Holy Spirit will bring to mind other people or events that need to be forgiven. Write those down so that you can go back to them when you finish the current forgiveness statement. Because our bodies and minds have intertwined the various hurts, it is also likely that you will jump from one person to another and then back again as you work through the forgiveness process.

The person hasn't changed their behavior

It is very difficult to forgive when you know the person is going to offend again. Yet, we don't find an exception in Scripture allowing us not to forgive due to the other person's continued actions. When Peter asked the Lord how many times we are to forgive our brother, Jesus' response was, "I do not say to you seven times, but seventy-seven times." (Matthew 18:22). Some translations say "seventy times seven," indicating that Jesus was saying to forgive without limit.

While hard, we need to forgive each offense, even if the offender is likely to continue the hurtful behavior. The reality is that as we forgive, we will start to see them differently. As we see them more clearly, the new offenses will have less power over us. Forgiveness is like putting on a protective coating that makes the messy stuff less likely to stick to us, like a Teflon pan; it can just slide off.

That is not to say that their continued harmful behaviors are okay or acceptable. It is possible that you will need to make adjustments to remove yourself from being easily available for the offender to hurt you. Each situation is unique and needs to be evaluated independently. Find a safe person who can help you to see the different aspects of the situation and help to determine what is best for protecting you from future hurts.

Demonic influence

When it is extremely difficult to forgive and remain in the fruit of that forgiveness, it's time to see if there is an extra layer of spiritual attack present. Demonic influence may be present due to a generational sin or curse. We won't go into detailed teaching here. For more you can read our book *Behind Enemy Lines: A Discipleship Course in Spiritual Warfare*.

Sometimes, demons travel in teams and carry names similar to emotions. Unforgiveness, bitterness, and pride can reinforce each other and make it more difficult to overcome an offense. More difficult, but not impossible. All things are possible in Christ Jesus.

Reflection and Review

Which of the hurdles tend to be the most difficult for you to overcome?

Do you have a particular individual who triggers emotional time travel for you on a frequent basis?

Do you need to find a trusted pastor, counselor, mentor, or friend to talk this through?

Section 2
Grief

6

Grief and Loss

We have chosen to combine our writing on forgiveness with grief and loss because they are so interconnected. Remember the story at the beginning about having to forgive the denominational leaders? We did so during a period of profound grief. We were still grieving a huge personal loss within the family, and then, we had to grieve losing our community when we were forced out of the church.

Contrary to popular belief, grief is not limited to processing the death of a loved one. We grieve anytime that we experience a loss, any loss. There can be deep wells of grief which must be processed with broken relationships, chronic health conditions, the loss of employment, or even the death of a dream.

We can grieve things that we hoped would happen that didn't. This relates to expectations we had of ourselves that don't materialize, such as life aspirations or professional goals. We may grieve the absence of a significant figure in our life for momentous occasions. Sometimes, this is due to scheduling conflicts or differing priorities; other times it is due to the individual being deceased.

We do not grieve as those without hope

We live in a fallen, sinful world, where death and loss have a bite that hurts like a scorpion. The sting of death is real, and yet, it does not get the final say (see 1 Corinthians 15:55). Through Christ we have the victory. However, we have to choose to walk in Christ's victory, removing the sting of death from our life.

The first step in walking in victory is to accept Jesus Christ as our personal Lord and Savior. If you have never done this, we encourage you to reach out to us, and we would be thrilled to introduce you to Christ. It will forever change your life here on earth and for eternity.

"But we do not want you to be uninformed, brothers, about those who are asleep, that you may not grieve as others do who have no hope." (1 Thessalonians 4:13). Paul goes on to talk about a believer's hope in the resurrection of those who have died in Christ. As believers, our hope is in Jesus Christ.

How are we then to grieve? The depth of bereavement can be intensified if we are a believer and our loved one is not, or there is an uncertainty of their choice. There is a difference in the way we actively grieve because of the understanding of the eternal significance of choices made. Regardless of our loved one's decision, we work through the grief process with the help of the Holy Spirit. If we become overly focused on our sorrow, we can become overwhelmed. While our losses are real in this world, the Lord is greater. He has hope for us that we can cling to today and in the days ahead.

God comforts us in our grief. He likewise expects that we will comfort others in their losses (2 Corinthians 1:3-7). Comfort does not take away the hurt, rather it takes us through to the other side. Psalm 23 is a Scripture that we can hold onto as we walk *through* the valley of grief.

Grief is a process

Grief, like forgiveness, is a process, although not a linear one. There are multiple components which all need to be addressed.

Grief is a strange process. There are moments of joy in the remembrance, lack of hope in not having control, despair in the loss, alternating acceptance and denial of the reality of the situation, and experiencing anger in the outcome or even the process. We can have moments of rational thoughts that quickly morph into the irrational. We call this the Emotional Web of Grief and will take a deeper look at it in chapter eight.

Many of us like cut and dry, black and white, right and wrong, definite answers. The grief process offers almost none of those things. Will it last a few days, weeks, months, or years? Emotions flip from one to another without warning. Routines are out of whack. Things just don't seem to be right.

Time and healing

While time removes you from the intensity of the initial feelings, it likely will not "heal all wounds" as the adage says. Time provides perspective and distance from the loss, maybe some numbness, but time itself is *not* a healer of wounds.

Mark's Mom passed away in 2006. While it has been many years since her passing, we still have moments of grief related to her not being here. As births, graduations, and other momentous events occur, we often wish that she was with us to join the celebration. There are innumerable times when we wish we could talk with her and get her perspective. Time has made it more normal not to have her around, and yet, the grief is still real, just not as heavy or debilitating.

Healing requires effort and work. When we are physically hurt, our body works to promote healing of the wound. When we are hurt by people, we get to choose to forgive and do the work of recovering, or we can remain in a place of hurt. A wound left uncared for, or one that is not able to heal, can turn worse or even deadly.

When we experience a loss, we need to do the work of healing. That work is done in the process of grief. It's easy to get stuck, but we must continue the process for as long as it takes.

The effects of grief

As we process through grief, it is helpful to put in systems for managing the day-to-day routines of life. Things that we used to do automatically may get missed because of the effects grief has on our minds and bodies.

> "It feels like being mildly drunk, or concussed. There is a sort of invisible blanket between the world and me. I find it hard to take in what anyone says." (C.S. Lewis, *A Grief Observed*, page 3)

When grieving, our brains don't work the way we are used to them working. Keeping our thoughts straight can be difficult. Even normal tasks take longer, become difficult, or may even become temporarily impossible because of the inability to maintain our focus and energy. We call this phenomenon "grief-brain". For most of us, grief-brain is extremely frustrating, and we may even feel like we are losing our minds. It is helpful to acknowledge the reality of the additional negative impacts of grief and its effect on our brain's normal processing. Once we are aware of these factors, we can implement tools to help us function.

When we are compromised with grief-brain, the rational and reasonable seem to go out the window. Seemingly meaningless things can become triggers that cause us to break down crying, often without warning. We may not seem to have an ability to control our emotions and how they are displayed. Tears, cries, shouts of anger, swings from one extreme to another, happy, sad, depressed, remembering, forgetting ... it may all be a jumbled mess. Grief-brain is real. Recognize it and don't beat yourself up when it rears its ugly head.

There is a physical component of grief. When grieving, we may lack the drive or ability to function. This will impact even the seemingly mundane tasks of the day, such as eating, bathing, or dressing. We may lie on the couch feeling cold, knowing that if we just got the blanket from the other end we would be warm, and yet there is an inability to move enough to get the blanket and spread it across yourself. Having someone around to help you with even the simple tasks can be important.

Our current grief may be exacerbated by grief from prior losses. We talked about emotional time travel in chapter three; it applies to grief as well. When we have unhealed places, the injury of loss triggers those prior hurts. It is important to work all the way through the grief process, including addressing any needed pieces of forgiveness that we discover along the way, so that it doesn't come back to bite us in the future.

Interacting with others

It can be awkward to interact with others when we are grieving, as well as for others talking with us. How much do we say? What is an acceptable response to their offer of condolences? What if they don't mention the loss; do we act like it isn't there or attempt to initiate a conversation regarding the loss?

It is difficult to sit with another as they grieve, because it makes us uncomfortable. We don't know what to say or do to help them. Honestly, your presence is almost always more valuable than your words. When Job was sitting in ashes grieving, the best thing his friends did was to sit with him in silence for the first seven days. It was when they started to speak that problems occurred.

Words are not what is most needed when someone is grieving. They need your presence; someone to sit and be with them in the depth of the loss. Often we speak out of our discomfort and say things that actually make it harder for the person we want to help.

After the passing of Mark's dad, a gentleman from church, upon hearing about the loss, simply stepped up to Mark and gave him a hug. This was a powerful moment for Mark. There were no words that could have been said to equal the impact of that hug.

When we are the one who is grieving, it is a mixed bag to talk about the loss. There is healing in the process, and yet, we don't want to impose our struggles on others. It seems unfair to expect another to carry a portion of the weight of our grief, even if only for a short time.

It may surprise you, but even professionals who help others process through grief need someone to help them. None of us are fully able to go through the process alone. It is great if you have a friend or family member who can talk with you. If there isn't anyone close, or if your grief is especially deep, you may need to seek professional assistance. There is absolutely no shame in asking for help.

Isolation is a tool of the enemy to bring us into his pit of despair. He will often use guilt, insecurity, or embarrassment, to cause us to withdraw from those we need the most in our process. Two are better than one as we are able to lift each other up (see Ecclesiastes 4:9-12). We need each other, especially in the hard times.

Things that we grieve

There are many things that we will grieve throughout our lives. Any loss that we experience will require some level of grief processing. What are some of the things that we may experience and have to grieve?

Grieving a death

Most of us know about having to grieve the loss of a loved one or pet. Experiencing the death of a close friend or family member is usually a socially acceptable time to actively grieve in most societies. The biggest shortcoming of expectations that we generally see in our culture is the time allowed to grieve. We'll take a deeper look at each person's individual grieving process, including time, in the next chapter.

Not all deaths impact us the same way. A child may need to grieve the loss of their beloved goldfish while others will not be impacted at all. Generally, the closer you are to the person or animal that died, the deeper you will experience grief. Give yourself permission to grieve each death as you need.

Some deaths may hit you with an intensity of grief that you were not expecting. Mark and his dad were effectively estranged for several decades. Mark grieved his relationship with his dad for years and thought that when he died there wouldn't be much left to grieve. To his surprise, the grief was much deeper than anticipated, and manifested in ways that were not like a "normal" death. Just because you have grieved a relationship does not mean that you have grieved the death of the person.

Something very few people realize in grieving a death is that we may have to forgive the person for dying. We discussed this in chapter three if you need to go back and review.

Grieving what could have been

This one may be a bit less obvious for many, but it really is grief. There are times that we will need to work through the grief of missed opportunities or dreams, even when what we got was better.

In 2015, Mark was working on a plan for growing his CPA practice in a way that would fund our living and allow for the time of establishing and growing the ministry that the Lord placed in our hearts. It was a good plan, and Mark was looking forward to watching it come to fruition. Then, out of the blue for him, the Lord asked that we sell the business and jump right into full-time ministry. By saying "yes" to the Lord, we lost what we were looking forward to in the future. What the Lord has for us is beyond imagination, and yet there are days that we still wonder what it would have been like to experience the original plan. Grief has been a part of our process.

Most of us have dreams about the future. Some of those dreams may come to fruition, but many may not. These dreams will vary as each of us is different. There may have been a dream about where we would live, how many kids we would have, what adventures we would experience, or any number of other things. When we realize that our dream will not come to be, there is a need to recognize and grieve that loss.

Grieving not having a relationship to grieve

There are many of us who have strained or non-existent relationships with parents or other family members. These may be caused by premature deaths, individual choices, or uncontrollable circumstances. Regardless of the cause, we grieve the missing relationship.

We know of multiple individuals who went through a divorce and nasty custody battle. In spite of all of their efforts, the courts ruled in a manner that required entire family units not to have any contact with the children. Those impacted by the orders have spent years grieving not having those relationships.

Another example may be grieving not knowing a biological parent who gave you up for adoption. It is common for adopted kids to wonder what it would have been like to grow up with their birth parents. They also frequently deal with feelings of rejection or inadequacy. Grieving the lost relationship is a part of the process of being healthy, even if it is possible to connect with each other later in life.

Pastors and their families may grieve the isolation that can come with ministry. Being set apart, or looked up to, can place expectations on the ministers making them feel like they cannot be as real and authentic as they would like to be. This can lead to feelings of loneliness or isolation. The children may misbehave as an act of protest for the expectations they don't see placed on other kids.

Letting go of things we've done

Similar to grieving things that could have been, we will often need to grieve the things that we have done and are no longer doing. This could be because of physical limitations such as no longer being able to play a sport we enjoyed or living independently.

Through our life, we will have to let go of many things that we have enjoyed. In our work, we may change careers or employers, leaving behind the prior job and all that it entailed. It's possible that we developed programs that one day come to an end, or we have to pass it to someone else to continue. A mother who stayed home to raise her children will have to grieve them growing up and leaving the house, leaving her to find new purpose and activity in her daily life. All of these situations may result in having to process grief.

A friend was telling Mark about a program in his ministry that he developed and managed for the prior five years. It was his baby so to speak. The ministry has grown to the place where this program needed to be passed to someone else to continue while Mark's friend worked in other areas of the ministry. He described it as feeling like a chunk of flesh was being cut off him; a part of him was being removed and taken by another person. While recognizing that it was a good thing to do, the process of letting go was difficult. He had to grieve that he would no longer be running that program.

When missionaries leave their assignment, and home, in a foreign country at the conclusion of their ministry, there can be a grief that the impact of their labor is intangible. They may also grieve the change in situation including familiar surroundings, cultural food, friends, and responsibilities. They will need to grieve all of these changes, somewhat simultaneously.

Grieving our own actions

There will be times that we will need to work through forgiveness of ourselves and then have to process the grief associated with the result of our own actions. This grief can look a lot of different ways. Let's take a look at some examples:

If you participated in an event that led to a death, such as an abortion, accidental death, or murder, there is the obvious forgiveness work that needs to be done. It is also important to work through the grief of the *results* of your actions. There was a loss of life that will likely result in grief for yourself and others as well.

Perhaps in your earlier life, you acted in destructive or harmful ways that were contrary to who you are now in Christ. You may have battled an addiction or another repetitive negative habit. You will likely have to grieve the time and opportunities lost due to your indulgence. If there are people who have been affected by those actions, then you may need to grieve the hurt that you caused. This will be more likely if the persons affected are close to you, such as children or family members. Even though you have changed, the effect of your prior actions may still be playing out in their lives.

How do you work through the grief for things that you caused? The first steps are granting forgiveness toward yourself, and asking for and receiving forgiveness from the Lord. After you have been forgiven, you will need to process through the various stages of grief until you have completed the work to be free from the burden of the past.

Unfortunately, you cannot change what was done, nor can you choose for others how they will respond, including their choice to forgive you or not. It may *seem* like you will never be free until forgiveness is received from those affected. However, if this is true, then the enemy wins. That is not how God works. God's grace is greater than other people's decision to forgive.

Being able to move forward in life does not mean that all consequences are removed or resolved. When King David sinned with Bathsheba, there were more immediate consequences like the death of the child conceived in the sin, as well as lasting consequences that affected his kids, specifically, Absalom. You can read the story in Second Samuel chapters 11 through 18. God forgave David and continued to use him as king, blessing the nation of Israel through him. However, Absalom and David did not resolve the issues between them, and the result was strife and difficulty in their relationship to the end.

We can choose to do our part in responding to the other person with humility, taking responsibility for our actions without excuses or justifications. If they respond with forgiveness, we have the opportunity to restore the relationship. If they choose to continue in hurt and unforgiveness, we will have to grieve the loss of relationship.

The above is just a sampling of things that we grieve. There are many, many losses that we experience in our life journeys. Recognizing the losses and working through the process of grief will give us freedom to move forward into new things. When we fail to grieve properly, it is possible to be weighed down and not even realize its effect on our emotional state. This can result in not being fully effective in our current and future activities.

Reflection and Review

What losses am I still grieving?

Who do I need to forgive related to unfinished lingering grief?

Am I grieving anything related to my expectations and disappointment?

7

Individual Process

You are unique. God created you that way. The way you process grief and the timing of that grief is also individualized. Couples, families, and those that suffer an organizational loss will not respond exactly alike. Be diligent to offer those around you the opportunity to grieve as they need rather than forcing them into your experience or expectations.

Grieving your way

It is important to give ourselves permission to grieve in the manner and timing that we need. There is no one *right* way to grieve.

When a family experiences a loss, there is often a coming together and support for each other. There is also a tendency for all family interactions to center around the loss for a time. However, there comes a time when all involved need to move past the loss being the center of attention and choose to go on living after a passage of time. This does not mean that the family stops grieving. The grief may linger; it just won't continue to be the central theme of the relationships and interactions.

Many losses in a family will result in similar grief responses. The loss could be the death of a family member, a divorce, loss of a job or ministry position, a member choosing to adopt a lifestyle contrary to family values, the loss of a foster child through new placement, a miscarriage or abortion, etc. The reality, though, is that similar responses do not guarantee the same pace or synchronized processing of grief elements.

Each family member will respond to the loss differently, even though it is a shared experience. We need to give permission to ourselves and others to work through the grief at our pace and in our way.

Mark has three siblings. When their mom died in 2006, and then their dad in 2021, the deaths affected each one differently. It is easy for someone from the outside to look at the siblings and say that one is doing well while another is *not* managing the grief well, solely because it looks different. The truth is that each is in their own place in the process.

Even within a married couple, there will be differences. Dallas was enrolled in graduate school to earn her counseling degree when Mark's mom passed away. While she stepped away from her studies briefly, it wasn't long after Judy's death that Dallas took a course in Grief and Loss.

Mark was very close to his mom, as was Dallas, so the depth of grief was significant. Dallas grew increasingly concerned as she watched Mark in the following weeks and months. There was a seeming lack of acknowledgement or response to the underlying and undeniable lingering grief on Mark's part.

Concern turned to anger, because Dallas couldn't understand how she could be having such a difficult time while Mark was going through his normal routine. It took a while for her to remember that her professor had advised that each person would grieve in their own way. Then, somehow it came up in conversation that Mark actually had to pull off the road so he could scream and cry without being a danger to anyone around him.

Privacy was important. He didn't want to grieve in front of Dallas because his outlet was such a demonstratively passionate outpouring of grief. He didn't want to scare her, or make her load heavier to carry.

Eventually, Dallas understood and accepted Mark's need to grieve this way, without any expectations of completing her mentally constructed checkboxes. She was able to forgive him for not walking through the process the same way she was. This was a turning point which permitted us to support each other better through the remainder of our grief journeys.

As you see in the above story, the different ways we grieve may cause conflict with the people around you; especially those closest to you. When you need each other most, the grief can get in the way of your relationship. It is important to recognize what is causing the conflict, then to talk about where each of you are in the process. This discussion should be filled with grace, for each other and yourself.

Forgiveness will likely be a part of the process. Some of the things we may need to forgive are: people for not understanding us in our grief; peers for not recognizing why we are grieving; and a lack of empathy for the depth or duration of our grief.

In addition to giving yourself permission to grieve uniquely, it is important to allow those around you to grieve in the manner that they need. There should be no space for judgement. Every person has to do their own work. No matter how much we want them to get better, they get to choose at what pace, and in what manner, they will grieve.

However, this is not an excuse or permission to stop working and get stuck. If you, or a loved one, are stuck in the grief process, find help from someone who can assist you in getting things moving again.

Loss of support system

In contrast to experiencing a loss where the family unit can support each member collectively, is the grief and loss experienced by church leaders or members when they are cut off from a church body. Regardless of circumstances, any removal due to unresolved conflict results in an abrupt loss of an entire support system.

Their friends, which became family by choice, and their spiritual community largely involve the same people. In such instances, the individual and their family are left to grieve in isolation. While they may be able to gain support from a spouse, the partner is also grieving and can only provide a diminished amount of emotional reinforcement. They are each grieving the circumstances that led up to and caused the breach, as well as, the multiple losses of friendships and familiarity. In these cases, even the daily routine is compromised.

While it is hard to imagine, there is the possibility of something good coming out of such a season of intense grief. Time spent lamenting before God can become time building intimacy in our relationship with Him. It is even conceivable that He will redeem the hurtful experience by growing us and building holy character and maturity.

As complex as the situation and grief may be, He is always true to His Word. As His beloved child, He will not leave you nor forsake you. He will guide you and be a lamp for your feet as you move forward one step at a time.

Pacing grief

Most of the world around you will continue like normal long before you are ready, or even able, to consider your life "normal" again. In fact, they will commonly expect you to be "over it" in a relatively short period of time. This may trigger an anger response in you and present you with additional opportunities to forgive.

When a royal or high official passes, there is an official time of mourning that varies by country. In our country, many companies provide bereavement days which can be used to miss work to mourn an immediate family member. These are usually very limited and do not correspond with the entire length of the actual grieving process.

It is important that you allow yourself the time that you need to grieve, regardless of other people's expectations. You also need to work on pacing your grief so that you keep moving forward, neither getting overwhelmed nor stuck in denial or avoidance.

With all of the emotions of grief, it is hard to consider how to manage it all, let alone navigate how to pace it. You will likely need help from loved ones and friends, maybe even a professional, to see that you are moving through the grief process in a good manner. Don't be afraid or embarrassed to ask for help; we all need it at times.

What does a healthy pace for grieving look like? While it will look different for everyone, the key is to be steadily moving forward. Some days that may be simply getting out of bed, dressed and fed. There will be times that you will have to force yourself to talk about the loss so that you don't get caught in the proverbial trap of burying the content that needs to be addressed and processed.

There will likely also be a few setbacks along the way. We can't let those cause us to quit working. Discouragement is common, and it is a method that the enemy likes to use to hold us down. When you sense that you may be getting stuck in one place, a shift may be needed to keep progressing.

Imagine driving on a muddy road. The mud is sticky and slick all at the same time. It can be difficult to steer the car and have enough traction to keep moving forward. The last thing that you want to do in this situation is to stop moving. When stopped, the vehicle can sink into the mud, making it much more difficult to start moving again.

If you've ever experienced such a situation, you know that there are generally three options for getting going; extreme power, backing up and trying again, or outside help. With the right equipment, it is possible for some to get unstuck by trying harder. Sometimes, you're able to gain forward traction by backing up and getting a running start at the sticky mud. Other times, you just have to call for help from others.

Whatever your muddy road of grief looks like, keep moving forward. Too much speed could cause you to go off the road, while not enough forward momentum may cause you to get stuck. A slow and steady approach is generally best.

Space

When we are in the midst of any situation, our vision can be skewed because of a limited perspective. This is especially true with grief. Much like when we are crying, which causes our physical eyesight to be foggy, the flood of emotions makes it difficult for us to see clearly and make the best decisions.

When Mark worked as a CPA, he would advise clients not to make any major decisions for the first year after losing a spouse. We believe that this advice is good for any significant loss experienced. People need time to be able to gain adequate space to be able to see clearly enough to make big decisions.

After we lost Mark's mom to cancer in 2006, he was in a compromised emotional state due to the intensity of the grief. We wish that someone had come alongside us and reminded us to hold off on major decisions.

She was a key employee in his CPA firm at the time of her illness and death. Her loss left him reeling, trying to determine if he should shrink the firm down to just himself with possibly a part-time assistant, or to grow it to be less dependent upon him for the everyday client needs. Within four months, he made the decision to expand and grow the firm.

In reflecting and looking back on it, Mark still believes that was the right decision; however, he did not go about the process in the best way. The decisions that were made in those months resulted in much difficulty in the succeeding years. He simply didn't have the full ability to see around him adequately in his compromised state of grief. Had we slowed down and allowed sufficient space, it is possible that many of the mistakes made in that time would have been avoided.

Anticipatory grief

There will be times that we anticipate a loss and start grieving prior to the actual occurrence of loss. Some examples would be when a loved one receives a terminal diagnosis, when we know that a move or change in position is forthcoming, role reversal with our parents, or even seeing our kids grow up knowing that they will be going off to college or moving out of our house.

While we haven't yet experienced the loss, we will begin to enter the grief process. We can choose to live in denial or start to work through our emotions. Recognizing that we are engaged in the more volatile emotions of grief, even before the culmination of the event, can assist us in establishing more realistic boundaries and evaluating the available emotional reserve to engage in relational activities.

Even if we are diligent to do the work in anticipation of a loss, there will still be grief when the actual foreseen event occurs. It is simply impossible to be fully prepared, or avoid a more intense response, at the moment of the finality of the previously pending loss. Watching someone fade away due to Alzheimer's or cancer forces you into a space of grief *during* the decline *and after* they are no longer living.

Common experiences

While each of our processes and experiences will be unique to us, there are some common things that many people experience as they grieve. Some of these experiences may make us think that we are losing our minds or are not doing it "right". Hopefully, you will see that the grief process is filled with strange reactions that don't necessarily mean you are on the verge of insanity.

You may "see" or "hear" the person or pet for a while

After our dog, Duchess, died, we would think that we heard her or saw her in the house. She was with us for fourteen years, so there were common routines and expectations that we had ingrained in our being that were suddenly missing. There were plenty of times that we would expect her to be under our feet, think we saw her black and white figure out of the corner of our eye, or we even thought we heard her collar jingle. Our mind was simply trying to fill in the void by using historically expected norms.

You may dream about them

Dreams are great places where we process things, especially losses. It is common to relive past experiences or future hopes that won't become reality in our dreams. We may also dream that the deceased didn't actually die. Of course, such dreams add to the difficulty of adjusting to the reality of them not being there each time we wake from that dream.

Disrupted sleep

A typical reaction to grief is depression, and a common symptom of depression is a disrupted sleep cycle. In other words, either you cannot sleep well, experience frequent waking throughout the night, or you feel like you cannot do anything except sleep.

Keeping to your evening routine and established sleep hygiene patterns may be the only intervention you need to get back on track in a relatively short amount of time. However, if you continue to struggle in this area, please speak with your medical provider regarding a possible short-term pharmacological approach.

Emotional instability

During active grief, one's emotions will likely be more volatile and unstable than normal. The highs will be higher and the lows will be lower. The cycle of emotions is commonly accelerated as we are grieving. We'll get into the Emotional Web of Grief in the next chapter.

Change of appetite

It is a familiar concept that emotional eaters will eat excessive quantities of food with no nutritional value to avoid dealing with the actual stressor(s) and response(s). During a time of intense grief, it is also possible that you will lose interest in food. Because our body requires nutrients from what we consume to continue functioning, it is important to eat when you would normally eat, even if you aren't hungry. Eating smaller portions is an acceptable accommodation, but skipping meals can intensify your emotional distress.

Triggering memories of prior losses

Emotional time travel is not only present when we deal with identifying forgiveness issues. It is also present in grief. The memory cues up bodily sensations which can become triggers in themselves for the last time we were grieving so intensely. Grief doesn't observe a predictable timetable. If you find yourself vacillating between memories of losses, give yourself permission to experience the memory, walk through the remaining grief from the past as well as the current circumstances you are grieving. Look for places where you may want to enter forgiveness work in the near future and record them in your forgiveness journal. If you tend to overfocus, set a timer and have a planned activity to help you exit your allotted time to grieve each day.

Less attention to detail

It is also common for a grieving person not to have as long or detailed of an attention span. This may lead to making silly errors on tasks. It can be helpful not to finalize a project on the first pass, giving yourself a minimum of a second look to catch mistakes. Depending on the importance of the task, you may also ask a trusted person to check the work. There may be days when you will have to postpone working on a detailed project if your attention is less than needed.

If your attention is compromised, please evaluate whether you are truly competent to drive in your current emotional state. We know a lady who stopped at a red light and then proceeded to drive before the light turned green. The officer who watched the events unfold told her he was confused about what happened, since he knew she had originally observed the indication to stop. Thankfully he understood when she explained that her mother had recently passed away. He let her go with a verbal warning and an instruction to go straight home.

Reflection and Review

Ways I am grieving similar to other family members or friends:

Ways I am grieving differently than those close to me:

Do I need to forgive anyone for grieving differently by time required or behaviors they are engaged in?

Which of the common experiences do I tend to experience?

8

The Emotional Web of Grief

There are various models of the stages of grief, and therefore, depending on the model, a differing number and description of the stages. "Stages" is somewhat of a misnomer, as one does not earn the right to progress to the next stage by completing the prior one. The tangled web of grief might be a more appropriate word picture as you cycle in and out and return to emotions and memories previously revealed by your unique grief journey.

The Kübler-Ross model uses five categories for the emotions of grief which we will explore shortly. Another frequently referenced model utilizes a deep U-shape with designations that start with Loss-Hurt on the left and work around to Loss-Adjustment on the right. We actually prefer the concept of the latter because it's easier to demonstrate a jumbled mess of emotions at any given time by simply scribbling between all the points in the middle.

We have experienced the jumbled chaos of the emotions associated with grief. Some of our losses have been the deaths of Mark's parents, being forced out of our church ministry, losing beloved pets, and of course other losses along the way. We write out of empathy, not just theory, as we have also journeyed through the Emotional Web of Grief.

A new way of looking at grief

We have taken the various concepts of stages of grief and developed our own illustration. We call it the Emotional Web of Grief. While we are processing any grief, we will be somewhere on the web of emotions. While only a few emotions are actually noted on the diagram for the sake of simplicity, there are many emotions experienced in grief. It is very common for us to experience more than one emotion at a time, as well as to switch between emotions, sometimes very quickly.

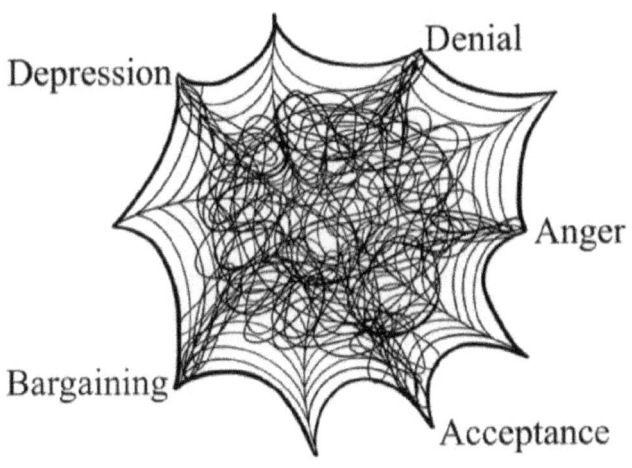

With all of the various emotions, it is important that we not get stuck in the "web" or process. The web can be sticky and difficult to navigate. Similar to a real spider web, getting stuck can lead to being eaten by the enemy. Our spiritual enemy wants nothing more than to destroy you. If he can accomplish this using your own emotions, he will.

Notice the random, crazy, squiggly lines going between emotions. Sometimes we circle and spin, seemingly without rhyme or reason. There is no set pattern to follow in the Emotional Web of Grief. It may be like a switch is flipped as we travel between two emotions. Other times, we may feel like we are stabilizing in one place.

As we move around the Emotional Web of Grief, we will spend varying amounts of time in different areas. We have found that spending too much time on any one emotion is a clue that more work needs to be done to free ourselves to continue forward. If we find that we are constantly in one of the emotions without moving towards a resolution of that emotion, then we may need help to get free.

While there are many emotions experienced, we will take a deeper look at the five most commonly recognized ones. They are anger, denial, bargaining, depression, and acceptance.

Anger

In processing a loss, we need to acknowledge the anger that we feel. Anytime we suppress our emotions, we are setting ourselves up for having to deal with them on a more explosive level in the future; this is especially true with anger.

Anger is one of those emotions that we generally think is bad or wrong. It is more beneficial to evaluate anger on the premise of how we engage it.

If the feelings of anger simply act as an alert that there is a problem or distressing factor present, it is operating in a space of encouraging us to engage in self-reflection and introspection. These activities guided by the Holy Spirit are productive and good as it leads towards growth, healing, and resolution. However, if we ruminate in anger and permit it to motivate us to act from a place of resentment, retaliation, or revenge, it becomes harmful to those around us, in addition to being harmful to yourself.

In chapter one, we provided the illustration of the anger iceberg. When experiencing the emotion of anger in grief, you may need to go under the water to determine what the root of the anger is to be able to deal with it adequately. More likely than not, you are angry about something other than the presenting issue.

Being angry at the person who died is common. It is also normal to experience anger toward the person or people whom we feel are responsible for our loss. There is almost definitely forgiveness work that will need to be done in each of these scenarios.

There are situations when we need to be angry for a little while before moving into forgiveness. This is okay and expected. While we don't want to stay in anger too long, it is also not healthy to short-circuit the process, as that could leave us with incomplete healing.

There is a tendency to be angry at the world for continuing to move on when you are in such distress and finding it difficult to operate at a familiar and comfortable pace. Recognizing the depth of your loss, while knowing that the people around you are not feeling it that deeply, is a starting place to deal with this anger. It is not reasonable to expect everyone around you to stop living because you have experienced loss. We may need to reevaluate our expectations of others and forgive them for not adequately acknowledging the depth of our emotions.

Denial

Some losses are easier to deny than others. However, with all losses, we will have moments when we want to deny that the loss occurred because it creates the need to adjust to something different. Change is hard. It's human nature to avoid it; however, long-term denial can create complicated grief down the road.

We often use logic to attempt to deny the necessity of addressing emotional content. Rationalizing or justifying why you don't need to examine how a loss makes you feel is a clue that you are engaged in active denial.

Denial can be less purposeful as well. Because of habits and routines, it is very easy to automatically think about calling a loved one to discuss something important or exciting. You may even be in the midst of walking to another room to tell a loved one you'll be right back, only to be jolted back into reality.

When Dallas' grandfather died, her grandmother was upset that the authorities had jumbled up all of his medications. Grandma was in the middle of reorganizing them when it suddenly dawned on her that it no longer mattered, because he didn't need those medications anymore.

Denial can give us a short reprieve from reality, but it doesn't last. The brunt of unwanted newness will eventually catch up to us.

Bargaining

If we can't have what we want, we will often try to obtain an acceptable substitution. When we experience a loss, we want to fill the space with something else. If we cannot find an acceptable substitution, we may try to give up something in order to get back what was lost. This is all part of bargaining.

See if this sounds familiar: "Lord, I'll (fill in the blank) if You'll (fill in the blank). This is a place of attempting to bargain with, or coerce, God into doing something that will immediately relieve the pain of loss, in whatever form we are facing it in the moment. While *many* have experienced this facet of grief, at the moment you are engaged in this exercise of mental gymnastics, you are the only one who showed up at the "bargaining table". God doesn't bend to our whims.

In desperate cases, bargaining may lead to some positive lifestyle changes. Think about the alcoholic or addict who realizes their choice to use a substance contributed to the dire circumstances of life altering consequences for themselves or others. Medical hazards can likewise attach in situations of severe behaviors, such as disordered eating, suicidal ideation, or unsuccessful attempts. Bargaining in these situations will typically involve a promise to abstain from future negative or destructive behaviors if a life will be spared.

Depression

We've previously mentioned some of the symptoms of depression. A general sense of blah and lack of motivation to do even the simplest of tasks can point to the fact that you may be on this anchor point of the Emotional Web of Grief. It may last for an hour, a portion of a day, or several days strung together.

It is highly unusual for someone to experience a loss and not have some depression. Part of depression is missing who or what we have lost. Before we can move to acceptance, we need to process the void. In Psalm 23, we are taken *through* the valley not *around* it. We need to go *through* the depression to the other side in our healing journey.

If it becomes severe enough to impede your ability to function in everyday life and mundane tasks in a variety of environments, home, work, volunteer activities, hobbies, etc. it's time to speak with a medical professional.

Unfortunately, some in Christian circles have determined, and teach, that any form of medicine, or at least those used to treat emotional or psychological issues, indicate a lack of faith in God. We don't believe it is a lack of faith. God created many natural substances used for medicinal purposes, even in Scripture. The key for us is who we are depending upon. The Lord may choose to use a medical doctor to aid us in our healing, even while we are walking in faith believing in Jehovah Rapha as our Divine Healer.

Acceptance

Acceptance is generally considered the last stage of grief; however, as with all the other "stages", you will likely move in and out of acceptance. Mentally knowing the reality of the loss is not the same as accepting it. Acceptance is not a perfect opposite of denial. We can know something, even believe it is true, and still refuse to have peace in saying that we accept it for us.

Mark had a business deal that went downhill. As he saw the events unfolding, there were attempts to salvage something, and yet it ended up with a large financial loss. When he knew that there was nothing else to do, he had to come to a place of acceptance. Yes, there was lots of forgiveness work to be done; there was the anger and denial of what happened, but the loss occurred anyway. The acceptance didn't come all at once. It came in a progression of heart changes. In the end, there was a peace from the Lord that He is greater than the loss incurred.

It is very common for people to think they have reached a place of acceptance and then discover otherwise. Expecting that we have reached the conclusion too early can lead to regression in the grief process. As Mark worked through the grief of the above-mentioned business deal, he had numerous occasions that seemed like acceptance, and yet, they were just a step in the journey.

Adaptation is acceptance plus adjustment and action. We are able to make adjustments in our life by taking actions that lead us to a new normal. Most of us do not feel we've exited the process of grieving until we have adapted well, and our new routines and reality feel more ordinary or automatic.

Emotional capacity

We have a limit in experiencing, storing, and expressing our emotions. When we are filled with various hurts, it is hard to be compassionate or caring towards others. Much like a physical room has a limit of how much can be put in it, we have a limit to our emotional capacity. In order to add and experience the good things that we want, we have to make space by addressing the undesired emotions.

Some of us just like to add rooms onto the house. Unfortunately, adding another room to a hoarder house that is filled with stuff doesn't change it from being a hoarder house. You have to clean out the junk to make space for living. The more rooms of stuff that you store, the longer the process can become of working through cleaning it up.

When we are struck with a loss, the emotions related to grief will fill a large part of our emotional capacity. In fact, the room will probably look like a tornado went through it, all jumbled and messy. It takes time for us to deal with each of the emotions, likely do some forgiveness work, clean and reorganize the room. When finished, the layout of the room will probably be different than before the loss. Regardless of how big the mess, we have to keep working to make it a place of functional living.

Anchored

Have you ever noticed that a web has to be attached to something? It has to have a basis of support, even though it is an architectural feat in its own right. As Christians, our emotional webs should be attached to our Heavenly Father. This provides security and assurance that there is more available than the difficult emotions we are currently facing.

When we are firmly anchored to the Lord, we will be able to navigate our Emotional Web of Grief with the hope that only He can provide. Regardless of how off-kilter we may feel, we can know that He is solid and dependable.

We've now looked at our unique process of grieving and how our emotions interplay with the reality of daily living. In the next chapter, we will take a look at some practical strategies to use when walking through grief.

Reflection and Review

Recognizing that <u>stages</u> of grief is a misnomer is helpful to me because:

As I look at the Emotional Web of Grief, I would say I'm at (name a placement).

As I evaluate my emotional capacity, I notice the following about myself:

9

Strategies for Grieving

It's one thing to talk about what grief is, the reasons we grieve, and the Emotional Web of Grief, but how do we practically work through the process of grieving? In this chapter, we will walk through actions that we can implement as we grieve. *Not every one of these strategies will work for every person or situation.* Adapting them to fit your personality and preferences will make them more effective for you.

Write it down; don't try to remember

As we discussed in chapter six, our brains don't work at peak effectiveness and efficiency when we are grieving. A helpful tool for dealing with grief-brain is to write everything down, even things that you would normally remember. It may be helpful to keep paper and pens at a number of locations around the house, so that it is easier to make a quick note. Consolidate the various notes into a central notebook daily and review them regularly. Alternatively, you can record them in your phone using your preferred app.

Letter of apology, forgiveness, or what you didn't get to say

"I wish I had been able to tell them (fill in the blank)". If you find yourself here in the context of needing to voice an apology, needing to express a hurt or disappointment, offer forgiveness, or even wishing you had shared things you enjoyed about the deceased as a way of encouragement, this intervention may help you.

It permits you to transfer your thoughts and feelings onto paper, or screen, rather than having to hold it in your mind and heart. It's a way to discharge some of the difficult content.

Side note: if you wish you had voiced encouragement, but didn't act on it, you may need to forgive yourself for missing the opportunity. This will help you move out of a place of regret.

Empty chair

We utilize this tool with clients in a variety of contexts. It works well for preparation for difficult conversations with family, friends, co-workers, and bosses, as well as forgiveness and grief work.

The basic premise is that the chair represents the individual you desire to address. Find a comfortable place to stand or sit facing the empty chair, then imagine the individual sitting across from you in the chair you've designated. Once you are able, begin to express your thoughts and feelings aloud.

If you are an external processor, you will probably feel more comfortable just talking out your thoughts as they occur and continue until you reach a place of natural conclusion. Even if you recognize you are beginning to talk in circles, it may prove helpful to keep verbalizing until you are more settled emotionally.

If you are an internal processor, you may want to spend time thinking through what you want to say when you are addressing the chair. If you are more comfortable reading something you have written ahead of time, that's permitted. The one thing we ask is that you actually read it *aloud* because additional emotional processing happens when you speak the words.

This tool shouldn't be rushed. Plan ahead and give yourself plenty of time and privacy to do the work you need to do.

Remember the lost in an appropriate manner

When we lose a loved one, it is important to remember them, and yet, how do we remember them? It is easy to distort who they were in life. This can lead to us living our life in a distorted fashion, almost as if there was a fantasy that becomes real as we live through the distorted lens we have created.

There is a tendency to want to not lose the memory of them. In this, we may overfocus on them and forget how to live our life. We can live as if they are still with us, and yet they are not. Leaving the bedroom untouched, as if they will return, is not healthy for our learning how to live in the new normal. The past is important, as well as the future, but they must not trump today.

Have we made any promises to the dead that we aren't able to fulfill, or in trying to fulfill them, we will lose ourselves? These types of promises can be detrimental. You may need to forgive yourself for making the promise and for not being able to keep it.

Remember them for who they were and what they did, the good and the bad. Nobody is perfect, so it is okay to recognize the imperfections of loved ones after they are no longer with us. Acknowledging their shortcomings does not diminish our love for them; it may even enhance our love.

Talk about it--the good memories and the hard ones

Talk with people who are willing to listen. At first this may be friends and family; however, over time they may tire of offering support in this way. Other suggestions to consider in this context of support would be a pastor, counselor, or even joining a grief support group for a time.

As you talk, share your treasured memories and funny stories. These are usually easier to access unless there is an element of unresolved circumstances requiring forgiveness work.

It is important to remember the individual in a more complete fashion rather than picking and choosing what to highlight in our minds. Therefore, we also need to talk about the hard stuff. Express the disappointments and frustrations as well as the good things.

Remember, you tend to romanticize someone as you talk about the good memories, their positive qualities, and the entertaining experiences shared together. Realistically, everyone has faults and things that are undesirable or even irritating. It's part of living as a fallen creature, even though as believers we are in a process of sanctification, working out our salvation becoming more Christlike.

Thank the Lord for the many memories and experiences that you were able to share

Part of talking about the good and bad memories is to be thankful that we got to have those experiences. Gratitude is good medicine for a grieving heart. Give thanks to God for the person or object that is lost. While we desire more time, we need to recognize the time that we shared and be thankful.

If it helps, make a list of the things that you are grateful for having experienced. This list can be a place to reference when you are feeling depressed to help return your focus to the positive.

Express your grief creatively

It is therapeutic to express our grief in a variety of ways. Some will benefit from looking at photographs, writing about the loss factually or in an analogous fictional way. Others will want to dance a mournful dance, play an instrument, or maybe even draw or paint their emotions. Verbally processing or singing songs that express what we are feeling can be other ways to express our grief. As each of us is unique, and our grief journey is ours, we should discover how we need to express and memorialize the loss that is beneficial to us.

Much like when we are cycling through the Emotional Web of Grief, we want to keep moving in the process. The danger of getting stuck in telling our grief is that we may end up reliving the loss in an unhealthy manner. There can be a downward spiral which takes us into an abyss of emotion and hurt leaving us stuck and unable to get out. It is vital that we express our grief in a way that allows us to rise up out of the emotional abyss. We need to eventually learn how to live again. Find activities that are healing.

Join a group

Sharing our grief with others in similar circumstances can be powerful. There is a camaraderie and kinship in sharing difficult experiences. There are focused support groups for those that have experienced traumatic losses such as the death of a child. It can be comforting to have people around you who understand what you are trying to express, even though you can't seem to find just the right words. Empathy is powerful as is sharing a similar burden. Helping others process their grief can surprisingly be therapeutic for ourselves.

If a support group isn't quite your "cup of tea," so to speak, see if there are shared interest groups at church that would be helpful. You need a safe place to begin to re-engage in activities of life. Perhaps this is a good starting point for you rather than continuing to process the loss. If you have lost your church or support system due to unusual circumstances, this coping strategy will require more effort on your part. When you are ready, look for community based groups through your library or online resources. In these cases, you will be in a unique situation of recreating differing levels of support.

Have realistic expectations

This isn't the time to make major *optional* decisions, including professional transitions, relocation i.e. moving away to avoid triggers, starting a new advanced academic pursuit, getting involved in a new serious relationship, or even attempting to establish healthier habits than you've previously engaged in. Strict diets, exercise regimens, and addiction detox also fall in this category. Likely, functioning in your basic routine is your best standard for expectations for the near future, as you will tend to revert to the most familiar during this season. For most situations, we recommend giving yourself at least a year before you start making big decisions. However, if you are forced to experience one of the above decisions, in addition to your initial grief event, be aware that it can elongate your adjustment period.

Take each moment as it comes

This goes along with having realistic expectations of yourself and others. Having structure is good, as it helps to keep you moving. However, don't plan too far ahead, because you don't know how you will be operating each day.

When you have a wave of sadness or other emotion come, allow it to be experienced. Give yourself permission to experience the plethora of emotions that will come. Don't shut down because it is uncomfortable. Likewise, don't dwell in the negative spaces. There is a need to emote and then get back to a place of functionality.

Often we will get so caught in the grief that we forget to enjoy what is in front of us. It's good to recognize the good that is occurring in life. Whether laughing or crying, we need to see the blessings and find joy in the midst of the pain.

Keep as much of your normal daily routine as possible; eat, sleep, exercise, and work with modifications

While starting a new diet or exercise routine is not typically advisable in the midst of grieving, keeping up with your established patterns and routines regarding eating, exercise, work, hobbies, and sleep will help you get through each day.

Our bodies have needs, and self-care is extremely important as you grieve. Following your normal routines gives you a sense of predictability. If attending church is part of your predictable routine, and you need to ask a friend to sit with you, please do. While you may choose not to attend during the intense portion of your grief, please add this back into your routine as soon as you possibly can.

Be aware of possible trigger dates, places, and special events

This is especially important in the first year. The first holidays, birthdays, anniversaries, and many other firsts are difficult, and sometimes, they will blindside us if we aren't aware. Don't schedule tests or other difficult things for these days. Prepare yourself for the possibility of your emotions to be compromised.

Triggers can happen out of the blue. We shared earlier that Dallas was in a grief and loss class shortly after Judy passed away. There was a particular class session that Dallas just couldn't hold herself together. She cried off and on for the duration of the three hours. On her way home, she was mentally composing an email to her professor to apologize. All of the sudden it struck Dallas that the date was exactly three months since her mother-in-law's death. The date itself seemed insignificant on the calendar, but to Dallas' body and brain it was *hugely* significant.

Ask for help

Your friends really do want to help beyond attempting to provide comfort and a listening ear. Meals are just one expression of this, but the reality is you can only eat (and store) so many casseroles or take-out.

While those who care about you want to help, usually, they just aren't sure how. Have someone help you create a list of things that need to be done that could be delegated. Then use this list when someone asks if there's some way they can help. Such a list may help alleviate potential frustration of having your mind go completely blank when someone asks how they may assist you.

Maybe you need someone to take your kids to the park so you can make some phone calls without being interrupted. Need a little help around the house catching up on dishes, laundry, maybe even your floors? Ask a friend if they can come help for a couple of hours. Perhaps they can help by picking up a grocery order or prescriptions so you have fewer errands to try to remember. Each of these suggestions also helps you conserve your limited amount of energy for the higher priorities.

Creating a memorial

The most obvious ritual and memorial after the death of a loved one is a funeral, and for some a wake. These observances help those left behind acknowledge the finality of the situation and begin to walk through the adjustment process.

Some find that these occasions are not sufficient, and they need an additional remembrance to be observed each year on the date of significance. Do you want to get together with specific individuals annually? Do you want to visit a specific place annually as a memorial? Engage in something that is fulfilling and meaningful to you as you move forward in life.

Allow yourself to cry and yell

We know from experience that there are some of you that think it just isn't okay to cry or yell. If that's you, we encourage you to verbalize permission for yourself to utilize these emotional expressions. At times, the only adequate release is to cry or yell. In regards to deep grief, you may find yourself wailing which is best described as a combination of a deep guttural cry and yell melded together. It is preferable to find a place where you won't alarm anyone in the vicinity.

Stuffing your feelings will cost you. It really is a "pay now or pay later" type of dilemma. Of course crying and yelling now does not mean you may not need to do it again further into the jumbled emotional web, but rather it means that you're in the midst of the process, rather than avoiding it.

Mourn the loss of future experiences with our loved one

Part of our grief is the loss of future experiences. We need to recognize that these will come, sometimes unexpectedly. Some obvious future losses could be marriages, the birth of grandchildren, and graduations. Less predictable future losses may be a conversation or just the comfort of being together.

As we grieve the loss of a loved one, we don't want to package all of the future into the present. That could be overwhelming. We need to recognize that those moments will come, and grieve them as they arise.

There is hope

We have shared some of our past acquaintances with grief in our daily living blogs on our website, but perhaps it will help you to revisit a portion of one of those here. This excerpt is taken from the blog written after our dog,

Duchess, died and originally posted on our website January 24, 2020 under the title, "When It's Time to Say Goodbye".

I (Dallas) know the theory. I've walked with clients through it countless times, but the knowledge doesn't give me a pass. I still have to walk through the days of countless tears, tripping over unexpected triggers, verbalizing the fun memories as well as difficult emotions, eating only because it's time to eat, and writing everything down just so that I'm somewhat functional despite my intense brain fog. Each day gets a little easier to face when I awake, yet again, to the reality of having to adjust to a new normal/new routine without her.

Because I've been down this road before with loved ones and beloved pets, and because I've walked with others through it, I know that the depths of this grief will not last forever. I offer you the same hope.

Reflection and Review

Who would I trust to help me if they asked what they could do?

Do I have a trigger date in the near future that I need to be aware of?

Two strategies I want to start using this week are:

10

Trauma

In this chapter, we'll look briefly at trauma. The story below *(set apart by italics)* is an account of a traumatic rollover accident our daughter experienced. If you feel you may be vicariously traumatized by reading her account, please feel free to skip those sections.

June 24, 2016. That was the day that turned me upside down…literally. If you were riding in my vehicle with me on the interstate that morning, you would have been upside down, too. That's because I was involved in a rollover accident, and yet, despite the terrible damage that my beloved car sustained, my Lord and Savior covered over me and kept me completely unharmed.

Backing up just a bit to catch you up to speed, I got on the interstate and was behind a white van. Pretty soon, the white van passed a white car and then it was my turn to pass. I got over into the left lane and began accelerating. I was almost parallel with the white car, with me still slightly behind the front of the white car. As I continued, I saw it begin to cross over the lane line, and I realized that the white car was coming over into the left lane. And it didn't stop! It just kept coming over! I did all I could think to do: move as far over to the left as the road permitted so that they wouldn't hit me and to give them time to realize that there was a car there: me!

And then, just as quickly, my tires grabbed the gravel that met the shoulder and flung my car into the median. I was hoping that the deep, grass median would be my stopping place, but instead, I saw to my left that I was crossing the oncoming northbound traffic. (After the event, my dad and I pieced together that I had been travelling backwards at this point because I saw a red SUV and another car driving towards me out the driver's side window). After crossing the road, I reached the dirt shoulder of the northbound interstate, hit a fence, and flipped over in my car, landing upside down in the dirt, staring at a crushed and cracked windshield in front of me. The entire time from entering the median until seeing a pair of legs beside the car coming to the scene, I was crying out, "God, help me! God, help me! God, help me! God, help me!" I didn't know what to do. When my car stopped moving I realized that I had just been in an accident.

The first man I saw planned to cut me out of my seatbelt while I propped myself up to keep from falling, but then I realized that my hair was stuck under something. I was thinking, 'Not my hair! Please don't cut my hair!' Luckily, he was able to get my hair out from whatever was pinning it down without using the knife in his hand.

After grabbing my phone and purse and phone case, which had been strewn apart from each other during the tumble, I crawled out of my car through the back passenger side. I walked around the car to see probably close to a dozen people who had stopped and come to the shoulder. One of the most amazing and miraculous things that I have said so far is that I walked away from the bashed-in car! Two women came up to me and told me that they were nurses (they had been driving behind me) and so they did a preliminary check and gave me a bottle of water while waiting for the medics to arrive on the scene. The crash looked so bad on the outside that one of them had brought a sheet because she didn't know how much blood there would be…

Considering what had just happened, I felt pretty composed other than the adrenaline and shock *coursing through my body. My spine felt fine and nothing else hurt.*

Eventually, I saw my sister's car on the southbound road in order to turn around to get to the other side of the highway where I was. When they arrived and we began walking towards each other, I broke down. I bawled into my twin sister's shoulder and then my dad's before having to pull myself back together to go back to a policeman and write my statement. The white car never stopped, and I doubt that they ever knew that they had caused an accident.

Experiencing trauma

The word "trauma" brings different connotations depending on your life experiences. It could be an emotional trauma such as being bullied, or losing a loved one through divorce or death, or even losing a pet.

It may be in the context of physical trauma, such as a car accident, combat experience, or being physically or emotionally attacked. It is also possible that it exists in a spiritual arena. You may have experienced spiritual abuse at the hands of the occult, or you may have even experienced spiritual abuse in Christian circles. This may happen on an individual level or as a part of a larger group, such as in the context of being a member of a leadership team or part of a congregation.

Trauma is experienced when there is a real or perceived threat to one's safety and well-being. It can be a time-confined event or something suffered over a longer period of time. There may be lasting effects from either of these exposures.

The familiarity and use of the term PTSD may or may not be accurately applied by the general populace. The criteria used to diagnose Post Traumatic Stress Disorder (PTSD) is multifaceted and worth researching, however, it is not a focus of this work.

While a portion of this chapter will discuss a few interventions for how to address traumatic events, if you identify with any of the above and recognize that you have experienced trauma that remains unresolved, we encourage you to find a Christian counselor. If possible, it would be best to work consistently with a counselor who specializes in trauma in your local area.

Part of the Christian lifestyle is to live in community. The healing process is an area where community is vitally important. Isolation or an attempt to approach this solely as a self-help method will likely culminate in a lesser result.

Aspects of unforgiveness and grief can be tied to trauma. We may still carry deep wounds related to traumatic experiences. It can be much more difficult to enter a place of forgiveness when someone has egregiously harmed you. It may be easier for you to identify the portions that you already grieve. There are losses: the loss of trust, the loss of innocence, the loss of safety, the loss of independence, the loss of property, or the loss of (fill in your loss here).

It is important to remember that forgiveness is for your benefit. It releases *you* from continuing to be tethered to the one that harmed you. **It does not in any way say what they did to you is okay.**

The body's reaction to the memory of a traumatic event will mimic the biometric measurements that occurred in real time, such as increased heart rate and breathing. This concept is similar to emotional and physical reactions triggered by being angry or scared in a dream and the lingering effects after you have awakened.

Because our body keeps track of past events, you can be triggered, or emotionally time travel, at any given time. Sights, sounds, smells, tastes, and the sense of touch can activate an unresolved trauma that is wrapped up in your memories. It will help you to dissect the memory by acknowledging and processing the triggers, grief components, and identifying places where you need to address any lingering unforgiveness.

Emotional Arrest

Experiencing a traumatic event can cause an individual to emotionally arrest at the age they were when the calamity occurred. This means that even though the person continues to age chronologically and even mature in thought processes, there is a tendency to revert to immature, emotional behaviors more in line with the younger age. Ever see a 30 year-old act like a 5 year-old? This might explain why the disconnect in age and emotional maturity is present.

When this occurs, it is important to find the original trauma and work through the healing process. Most likely this will require assistance from a professional or other qualified person.

We will often find that we need to work through the years since the event, asking the Lord to restore what the enemy has stolen. God is the ultimate Healer, and we need His help to be completely whole. When we invite Him into the hurts of the past, He brings restoration.

A different person

After a trauma, the person isn't the same one you remember from before. In many cases, they will most likely *physically* appear the same; however, this makes it difficult to remember that their traumatic experience has forever changed them.

To help you better understand this principle, think about a soldier that goes off to face combat. The way they survive is to depend on heightened awareness of their surroundings. They bond with those on their team who are working together to identify potential threats. Not all of their team members will return from the mission, so they carry the burden of grieving in silence or stuffing their emotions. Without either of these coping mechanisms, the soldier's mental capacity to remain alert could be compromised. They simply don't have the luxury of the time and space to grieve.

Violent experiences involving a threat to one's safety operate the same way in day to day life. One can develop new adaptations to avoid triggers, they may experience survivor's guilt, or they may find themselves very angry.

New adaptations to avoid triggers

Altering driving or walking routes, specific locales, or even avoiding certain people are some typical ways individuals adjust their routines to avoid triggers. Sounds and smells are a little more challenging to address proactively, as they can seemingly come out of the blue.

In these cases, finding a way to reorient yourself as quickly as possible is necessary. Look for a nearby non-threatening object and begin to describe it to yourself using as many senses as possible. If a counted breath exercise is better at helping you regain composure, try breathing in through your nose for a count of 4, and out through your mouth for a count of 8 for several repetitions.

Survivor's guilt

Our daughter struggled with survivor's guilt, especially upon learning of a classmate's death in a similar accident. There is a part of our brain that has difficulty understanding why we are left to deal with the emotional aftermath of a difficult experience, while another individual didn't make it through alive. God is sovereign and ordains the number of days for each of us. Survivorship is a concept that cannot adequately be addressed in our limitations of logic.

Anger

Anger may be part of your reaction to the traumatic event(s) you experienced. If so, use the Anger Iceberg exercise to help identify why you are angry (see page 29). Then, work through each identified contributing situation.

Removing guilt and shame tied to trauma

It is common to feel a sense of failed responsibility in the context of traumatic events. This can then morph into unrelenting shame and possibly guilt. This may be true in a context of not being able to protect yourself or someone else.

When we deal with any shame associated with trauma, we do a shame removal exercise. Typically, the client will invite Jesus into a mental picture they "see", and they will give Him what represents the shame, whether that be an object, word, photo, written record, etc. Once the client has surrendered the shame, we ask them to watch what the Lord does with it.

It is astounding how personalized the Lord is with each of these encounters. We have yet to have a repeat visualization scenario, even if the circumstances of the trauma or shame are similar. God is really interested in meeting you uniquely to provide healing.

Shame isn't always attached to instances of traumatic experience, so when we only need to process the traumatic memory with a client, we do healing of memories. We'll use the continuation of our daughter's story to illustrate this concept rather than describing it theoretically.

> *That evening, my mom did some processing with me and had me go through each part of my drive and the crash in order to see where Jesus was in the car with me. And what I saw through this very hard process of reliving the accident was that from the moment I was pulled into the median and through the entire accident, Jesus had stretched his entire body up and over me, like a human rainbow, to protect me on all sides. When the car was pulled right-side up, you could clearly see that the driver's side portion of the windshield was the most caved in, and yet I was not hurt by anything. It didn't even take two full days afterward for my neck muscles to stop being sore. Talk about incredible! God saw what was going to happen and said, "No way. She's*

mine and she's going to walk out of this crash. You can't have her!"

The first two nights were difficult to sleep through as I kept running through the scenes of the accident in my mind, playing the "what if" game, and catastrophizing the incident as what could have been. I had several bad dreams related to car wrecks those nights.

Fighting back against re-experienced trauma

Sometimes, the trauma is re-experienced during sleeping hours in nightmares and night terrors. Your mind is attempting to process the information to a point of resolution. When the trauma is being re-experienced in the context of nightmares or night terrors, as a believer, you can take spiritual authority. If you are experiencing difficulty sleeping due to the above issues, you have the authority to pray and command.

There is a difference in these approaches. When you pray, you are asking God to intervene on your behalf. When you command tormenting spirits, you are standing covered in God's authority and demanding that they leave you and your vicinity. For more information, see our book, *Behind Enemy Lines second edition*, pages 119-127, 177-179.

I seemed to be doing okay come Monday, but then as I was scrolling through my Facebook timeline that afternoon, I learned that a student at my university had died in a car crash the same day that I was in mine. I did not know him other than seeing him around on campus, but I assure you I mourned for him and his family like I had known them for years. This led to another processing session with my mom, because I had to fight with feelings of survivor's guilt, relive the fear of my own accident, confront the reality of death that seems so far removed until it punctures our reality, and mourn for his family.

I learned about this tragedy right before my dad and I were going to drive down to the site of the miracle (the term my dad coined for it to give God, not the enemy, credit for the outcome), but after a bit I pulled myself together enough to sit in the passenger seat to ride down and face those feelings again. I let out more tears as I continued to struggle with the thoughts of what could have been and as I mourned the loss of my beloved car.

'So,' you ask, 'does this mean that if I ever get into a car accident or other type of terrible situation, God will protect me just like He did for you?'. Obviously, I cannot answer this for you; only God knows what your life story will hold… I have struggled with this: that God completely protected me, yet I can think of *several young adults who were in automobile accidents who had very different outcomes.*

The "why?" questions haunt humanity because life is never black and white; it is different for everybody. (Adapted from Shanielle Henslee's account, July 2016. Used by permission.)

We cannot explain why some people experience deep traumas in life and others do not. The reality is that we all will experience some level of trauma during our lifetime. Our trauma is as real to us as any other person's is to them. Comparison is not helpful in determining the validity of our hurts. There is hope in the Lord for healing from the effects of each traumatic experience.

Reflection and Review

To me, trauma is….

Have I experienced something traumatic that caused me to arrest emotionally?

A place I feel shame and guilt is…..

I'll meet with Jesus in (setting for mental picture) and ask Him to heal this.

11

Walking in Freedom and Grace

Once you gain freedom, you don't want to go back to jail. Unfortunately in life, there will continually be offenses and hurts that we have to deal with and forgive. It is important to remain vigilant about forgiving each and every one of those offenses.

We will also have a new view of life and others when we walk in freedom. We remember our past, but see things differently. With our freedom, we are able to help others gain their freedom through forgiveness.

Staying free

Forgiveness and grief are a lot of work, and we like to think that there is an end to it. Unfortunately, we are humans living among other fallen humans, and therefore, we need to continue to forgive, or work through grief, for the rest of our lives. That does not mean that we are bound in captivity, just that we have to remain aware and continue to work to stay free.

Any new offenses need to be addressed quickly so as to not accumulate. The quicker we forgive, the less impact the offense will have on us. When we allow a hurt to fester, it has an ability to grow. As soon as we are able, we need to take the power away from the hurt and forgive.

We can be duped into thinking that the little things can be dealt with later, or that we can keep the peace by avoiding it indefinitely. This is not actually the case. The small infractions can layer one upon another and become rather large. Either you deal with the offense quickly, even though it may cause temporary distress, to fully address the issue and be free of it, or you let it linger and grow, and become something much more difficult to deal with later.

A new view

Without all of the offenses (fences of unforgiveness), we have a purer view of people around us. One way we can recognize an issue has reached a place of complete resolution is that we get to see others as God sees them. A common way we see people we have fully forgiven is with compassion. We will often see their hurts and areas of need. God's love and grace is able to flow through us to others.

Clients also describe a seemingly tangible weight being lifted off their shoulders in some instances; other times they feel like breathing is easier. Each of these is simply an indicator of being able to move into freedom.

Forgiving is not forgetting

While it is possible to forget in some circumstances because of the healing God performs in our hearts, we do not *always* necessarily forget the events that occurred which led to the hurt. In our humanity, attempting to achieve an unrealistic expectation that there is a requirement to forget can create additional frustration. Unlike God, who *chooses* to forget our offenses (Isaiah 43:25, Hebrews 8:12, and other Scriptures), we aren't required to forget to indicate that our forgiveness is complete. We learn from both the good and the bad of the past.

While forgiveness and healing may provide a clean slate because the power of the emotional injury has been removed, we may still retain a "matter of fact" memory regarding the situation. The memory and emotions are separated during the healing process. Through healing and forgiveness, our past hurts become past events that are part of our story but no longer define our identity. Through forgiveness and healing, the situation loses its power over us, and our memories are simply a part of the historical journey that we have lived. The new found healing demonstrates more accurately who we are in Christ.

God is amazingly good at taking what the enemy meant for evil and using it for good. Joseph did not forget what his brothers had done to him (see Genesis 37:12-36), and yet, he had forgiven them and saw the hand of God in the process. After their father had died, the brothers were fearful that Joseph would retaliate.

> "But Joseph said to them, "Do not fear, for am I in the place of God? As for you, you meant evil against me, but God meant it for good, to bring it about that many people should be kept alive, as they are today." (Genesis 50:19-20)

We also see in Romans 8:28, "We know that for those who love God all things work together for good, for those who are called according to His purpose." This does not mean that all things *are* good. Paul is telling us that no matter what you have gone through, God is going to work it *for* good. Our testimonies are powerful tools in the Hand of God. There are times He may want us to remember the past so that He can work it for good in the future. The contrast of the two provides an opportunity for Him to be praised and glorified.

After a very deep and devastating ministry hurt, Mark spent a couple of years working toward forgiveness for each of those involved. One day, at a missions conference, Mark saw the leader, and possible instigator, of the events which resulted in the hurt. Previously, the mention of this man's name would have been enough for Mark to have a negative reaction. This day, after much forgiveness work, Mark was able to shake his hand and be completely at peace with him. It was then that Mark knew all of the hard work was worthwhile, and he had truly forgiven.

While we don't usually forget the event or have a memory wipe, you will notice the emotional distress will be lessened even to the point of being non-existent. This is one of the ways you know you have reached resolution and conclusion of the forgiveness process in any particular context or situation. It is remembered as a portion of your life story, your history, but it no longer grips or pierces your heart or stomach when you think about it.

A new normal (a.k.a. change)

Through all of life, we should be growing and changing. Our views of life and the world evolves as we learn and go through the variety of experiences that living brings. With loss, we are especially impacted in our paradigms and perspectives. Through the process of grief, we are changed and will never be the same again. We will learn to live in a new normal.

Take for example, a person who loses a limb. They will "heal" to the extent possible without that arm or leg. They will learn how to live life with the accommodations available and adjustments necessary to go about the everyday tasks of living. There will be days that they may not think about being short of a limb as much, but other days every moment may seem like a reminder of their loss. They will never have that arm or leg again, and yet, they will be able to live a meaningful life.

When we lose a loved one, we will have to heal to the extent possible and learn to live the new normal to its fullest. It will require work and effort to adjust, but we are able to do so. We will have reminders of our loss, but need not to allow those reminders to knock us out of living. We will never have that person in our life again, and yet, we will be able to live our life with meaning and purpose.

Helping others be free

When you see others struggle with unforgiveness or going through grief, you can be the instrument that the Lord uses to bring them to freedom. Take what you have learned and pass it on. Come alongside them with compassion and grace, helping them to see their jail cell for what it is. Then teach them how to use the key of forgiveness to get out of jail.

There is something about going *beyond doing* and entering into the realm of *teaching* that tends to help solidify concepts for us. Isn't that just like God to provide benefit for both the giver and receiver? It's also part of fulfilling the commandment to "Go, make disciples." Go, teach others there is more to forgiveness and more freedom awaiting them than they are probably aware.

Reflection and Review

Do I have any unaddressed forgiveness and grief?

How do I stay free?

How can I help someone else through their process?

Appendix

Common Questions about Forgiveness and Grief

What about the little things?

We've already instructed you to take thoughts captive and look for the details of the offending event as you compose your statements. So, yes, even the little things matter. It seems that the trite nature or feeling silly that we were hurt by something seemingly insignificant can trip us up. We want to believe we are better than that, or feed our image of perfectionism or martyrdom, which gets in the way of us stepping into forgiveness. If Satan can convince you that it's too small to address, he secures an access point because unforgiveness remains present. Additionally, little things can add up to big things in the context of emotional time travel. That motto, "No job too big or too small" applies here. Do the work … even if it's minutia detailing.

Are there things that are unforgivable?

Given that you are asking the question, it is likely that you have a deep wound that you feel would justify not stepping into forgiveness. God forgave Saul for killing Christians, so murder doesn't seem to be an exception. God forgave David for infidelity although He did not remove consequences. That would indicate that infidelity is forgivable. How about rape? Abortion? Abuse of a child?

The bottom line is that God doesn't look at differing grades of sin. Sin of any kind separates us from Him. We can be reconciled to Him through the perfect sacrifice of His Son, Jesus Christ. "Look, the Lamb of God who takes away the sin of the world!" (John 1:29). The only thing that can separate us from God is the unwillingness to accept His gift of eternal salvation. If God is willing to forgive, we should likewise be willing to walk into the place of doing the work necessary to forgive others of any and all offenses. Human to human there is no unforgivable sin.

By forgiving, am I giving the person a pass on what they've done, or implying I condone their actions?

No, you are not offering absolution or a removal of consequences. Forgiveness does not change a wrong into a right. You are shifting the responsibility of the administration of justice to the Lord. You can surrender your right to be offended, or hold an action or inaction against an individual, without offering approval of their decision and choice. No where in the process of forgiveness are you saying that what they did was okay.

Do I have to reconcile to complete the forgiveness process?

If you are using the desire or ability to reconcile to evaluate your success in forgiveness, you may be disappointed. Let's take a look at the Scriptural view of reconciliation as presented in our previous book, *Behind Enemy Lines*.

> Since reconciliation is not commanded, we can forgive without having to continue to be harmed. For those of you wondering about the instruction in Matthew 5:23-24 to "leave your offering at the altar and go and be reconciled," let's look a little closer at the relationship being described, as well as the word being translated as "reconciled." In this instance, you are the one who has offended another. In such circumstances, you are commanded to go to the other and attempt repair of the relationship by accepting responsibility and asking for their forgiveness. You are instructed to work toward change. The change may be an agreement to discontinue a relationship amicably, rather than continuing the separation with lingering angst.

The word used in these two verses is diallasso, and it is only used once in Scripture. It is a combination of the words dia and allasso. It communicates an expectation that you are to seek to repair a relationship (initiate a move toward change) even if you are innocent of all accusations. The Amplified Bible translates diallasso as "peace." Your role in the relationship is significant in the application of the term interpreted as "reconciled." There is a qualifier; inasmuch as it depends on you (Romans 12:18, Hebrews 12:14). The other person could make proceeding in peace impossible because of their behavior and attitudes. It still rests on you to conduct yourself in a manner appropriate for Christ's ambassador.

Reconciliation is important and may even be a part of the process of forgiveness. We need to seek the Holy Spirit's direction to know what He desires. The decision to reconcile is separate from the decision to forgive.

(Henslee, *Behind Enemy Lines: A Discipleship Course in Spiritual Warfare*, second edition, pages 74-75)

Is it okay to be angry as I process through the hurt towards forgiveness?

Yes. Anger is an alert system that you have something that needs to be addressed, whether dealing with forgiveness or grief content. In chapter two, we discuss using the anger iceberg to help you identify distressing emotions in relation to an offense. It is possible that you will use the same exercise as you grieve to discover items that you feel you've lost, whether realized or anticipated. One of the indications that you have completed the necessary work is that you no longer experience anger. The exception to this is a holy anger, but the emotional content will feel differently to you.

Is it okay to have conditions on forgiveness?

Do you want the same measure or condition to be used in evaluating your actions towards another person? Scripture says we determine our evaluation by the standards we impose. "For with the judgment you pronounce you will be judged, and with the measure you use it will be measured to you." (Matthew 7:2)

Conditions on forgiveness are not the same as boundaries on continued relationships. So, while we would unequivocally say it is not permissible to place conditions on forgiveness, we would also say it is completely appropriate and often even recommended that you renegotiate boundaries in your relationships once forgiveness has taken place.

How fast should I expect to finish forgiving?

This is a check-the-box type of question. It's not wrong to be curious, but the implication is that there is a right and wrong timetable expected. Each individual is unique and therefore the process, and time required, to reach the conclusion of the forgiveness work is variable.

Some wounds aren't as deep as others. You may have already begun the process of forgiveness on one matter while avoiding another altogether for fear of the length of the process. The only thing we can say is that the length of time to gain freedom and healing is not equal to the initial event. You can prolong the process, however, and that means you've chosen to delay your own freedom and healing.

I pray for them every day so I won't have bitterness. Is this the same as forgiving them?

It is great to be praying for our offenders; however, it is not the same as forgiving them. We still have to work through the process of forgiveness with every offense. The fact that you are able to pray for them with an honest intent for their good is a positive indicator that you are on your way to healing.

Remember that forgiveness is releasing our right to be offended. It is a specific choice that we make and a declaration of that decision. Even with the small stuff, do the work. As you forgive more and more, it becomes easier to stay clean of offenses. It's much like dusting the house. If you dust regularly, it is less work than if you let it pile up for years.

I think I forgave them. Why don't I trust them?

Trust is earned, not automatically extended. In other words, trust is conditional while forgiveness is not. We must come to terms that forgiveness is not measured in how much we trust someone moving forward.

When someone has broken trust, we have to assess whether it is healthy and safe to work to re-establish trust. If you find yourself being pressured by the other person to re-enter trust more quickly than you are ready, please evaluate whether or not you are in an emotionally or spiritually abusive situation, and make decisions accordingly.

What if the person is dead? Do I still need to forgive them?

Yes, you do. Remember, forgiveness is not for their benefit, but yours. Forgiving a person that is deceased is not the same as communicating with the demonic in which a dark spirit assumes the appearance of a loved one. Obviously, the latter is forbidden (Leviticus 19:31). This is a place where logic and emotion battle. Thoughts like, "They're dead; offering forgiveness is pointless." allows Satan the ground to continue to defeat you in the place of memories and emotions tied to this individual. It's not a little thing or a silly thing. Forgive them, even if they are gone.

Should I expect the offender to offer an apology?

This is a resounding, "NO!" You are responsible for your actions, alone. If you are waiting for an apology before you proceed, you are looking for a loophole to get out of what the Lord commanded you to do. If they offer one, be gracious in receiving it and extending forgiveness, but the expectation of an apology will likely lead you down the path of having yet another offense to forgive that particular individual for when it is not given.

When an apology is offered, how should I respond?

A common response to any apology offered is to say, "It's okay." The problem with that response is that what they did is *not* okay because it hurt us. Therefore, we should not say it is.

The best response is one that is sincere. "I receive your apology" is a good response. If you have already done the work before the apology is offered, you may be able to say, "I forgive you." When in a position that you aren't sure you are able or ready to receive the apology, you can answer with a statement like, "Thank you for apologizing."

Do I have to tell the person that I forgave them?

That depends. Are they approaching you and asking for your forgiveness? Then, yes, when you are able to genuinely say you are able to release the right to be offended, communicate that forgiveness to them. It is not required the instant they request it, but it may permit them to heal and be completely free.

If, however, you are the one to initiate the interaction with the intent of expressing your forgiveness towards them, please refrain. You are more likely to stir up more offense rather than putting it to rest. If you are approaching them with the secret hope or purposeful intention that they will offer you an apology, you are using manipulation to get what you want. Forgiveness and manipulation are from differing spiritual kingdoms. Check your true motives.

How does grief interact with forgiveness?

There are many places in the grief process that we need to do forgiveness work to move forward. We may need to forgive the person who died for leaving us. There is likely forgiveness required where we see that the situation could have been better, different, or expedited.

Much of the anger stage of grief will give us clues to offenses that we need to forgive. Who are you angry with and why? Therein lies the answer to who and what you need to forgive.

It is common to become stuck in the grief process because we don't do the forgiveness work needed. As you are grieving, look for offenses that you are carrying.

Is it okay to grieve as a believer?

Absolutely! To grieve is to experience emotions that God created for us as a part of being like Him. Our emotions are a vital part of who we are, and when we suppress them, we are choosing to live outside of a healthy life. This applies in all of life, not just experiences of loss.

As believers we grieve with hope in Christ, not as others without hope (see 1 Thessalonians 4:13). To experience loss and work through the plethora of emotions is not contrary to living in hope, provided that we do not allow the emotions to take us to a place of despair. As discussed in chapter eight, we move through the emotions so as to not become stuck in the web.

What is appropriate to say to someone who is grieving?

It can be awkward around people when they are grieving. We want to help and provide comfort; however it can be easy to step on triggers, or proverbial landmines for them. So what do we say? Silence is okay. In fact, sometimes being present with them in silence is the best thing we can do. Some of the most helpful days for Job with his friends were the seven days they sat with him in silence (see Job 2:13).

Sharing our empathy can be helpful to some and hard for others. We need to be careful that we do not minimize their loss or try to make our prior loss equal to or greater than theirs. Knowing that someone has made it through a similar loss may provide hope that they will get through the grief.

False hope is not helpful. Neither are statements like, "it will be better tomorrow," or "it's all going to be okay." It isn't all going to be okay. There is a significant loss that can never be replaced.

A conversation between a newly widowed woman with one who had lived without her husband for several years was overheard at church one day. The newer widow was asking how long it would take until she was used to being alone. The more experienced widow offered a rather blunt reply. "You never get used to it. It just gets a little easier to bear over time."

Our only true hope is in Christ; all other hope has a potential to fail us. In the midst of grief, it is hard to even see that hope at times. Talk about the Lord's goodness in ways that they can receive in that moment.

It is always helpful to prayerfully ask the Lord to give you the right words to speak. We also like to add to the prayer that the Lord keeps us from saying things that are hurtful or not helpful. The principle, "Less is more" generally applies when talking with someone in mourning.

When will I know that I'm done grieving?

Depending on the depth of the loss, it may take a lifetime to work towards completing the grieving process. As we do the work, the grief should become easier in the day-to-day functioning of our life; however, some things we will never truly finish grieving. That does *not* mean that we will continually remain at the same level of grief as time passes.

It's been fifteen years since Mark's mom passed. We have made much progress in grieving our loss of her presence; however, there are some days that the noticeable void is still there. Triggers, such as special events, can cause us to experience her loss anew. When this occurs, it is important to recognize our reaction and process those emotions.

As we grieve, our goal should be moving forward and not getting stuck in the process. We will learn how to manage the grief, not allowing it to rule us. If you find yourself in the same place of grief again and again, then you may be stuck. Outside assistance is often needed to get unstuck and continue healing.

It is important to have realistic expectations of the length of time and process of grieving. To think that we will take a few days, weeks, or even months, to grieve a significant loss is setting ourselves up for disappointment. The greater the loss, typically, the longer the process.

What do I do when God is silent?

In the depth of our grief, we may feel like God is silent. This can be extremely hard to bear. It may seem like He does not care about our loss or even about us. In these times, we need to be reminded of Who God is and that He is a loving Father. It is out of His character not to care.

While on the cross, Jesus cried out, "My God, my God, why have you forsaken me?" (Matthew 27:46b). In this moment of greatest agony for Jesus, His Father was silent. But the silence did not last, for we know in the next chapter that Jesus was resurrected and talking about going to the Father.

We do not have a nice easy answer for why God is silent at times. What we can offer is that based on Scripture, we can know that He cares for us completely and will never abandon us (see Hebrews 13:5). In those times of silence, continue to seek Him and press into who He is.

Blue Fire Legacy was established to support struggling and hurting ministers, missionaries, and their families in addition to equipping the Body of Christ. The ministry is solely donor supported.

To request services or to schedule speaking or worship leading engagements, please contact info@bluefirelegacy.org.

Blue Fire Legacy
PO Box 1557
Westcliffe, CO 81252
(719) 382-9518
www.bluefirelegacy.org

Devotional Blogs

Stories to strengthen you and encourage you in your faith delivered to your email inbox every 2-3 weeks.

E-Newsletter

Stay up to date with us and the ministry activities. The e-newsletter is delivered to your email inbox every 4-6 weeks.

Sign up on our website
www.bluefirelegacy.org/resources
Both resources also available on our Facebook page

Also Available

GET YOUR COPY
TODAY

www.bluefirelegacy.org/resources

www.ingramcontent.com/pod-product-compliance
Lightning Source LLC
Chambersburg PA
CBHW031145160426
43193CB00008B/254